Adventure Sports

ADVANCED
WINDSURFING

Adventure Sports

ADVANCED
WINDSURFING

FARREL O'SHEA

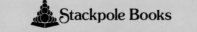

Stackpole Books

Cameron and Kelker Streets • P.O. Box 1831 • Harrisburg, PA 17105

A STACKPOLE BOOK

First published in Great Britain by
Salamander Books Limited,
London 1989 © Salamander
Books Ltd.

ISBN 0-8117-2303-8

Published by Stackpole Books,
Cameron and Kelker Streets,
P.O. Box 1831
Harrisburg, PA 17105
1–800–READ–NOW

Project Manager: Ray Bonds
Editor: Roseanne Eckart
Editorial Consultant: Brian Hart
Designer: Rod Ferring
Colour Reproduction: Scantrans
PTE Ltd., Singapore
Filmset: Flairplan Ltd.
Printed in Belgium by Proost
International Book Production,
Turnhout.

Dedication

For my mother, Anne. My sole inspiration in hours of need and
an example which I'm trying hard to follow.

The author
Farrel O'Shea is a professional windsurfer, sports consultant
and journalist. He started windsurfing in 1983, learning on lakes
and ponds and quickly progressed to shortboard sailing. He
turned professional in 1986 following a trip to Hawaii. Farrel is
the only British sailor, and one of the few worldwide, to
compete in the world's two most prestigious wave and speed
events – The O'Neill Wave Classic in Hawaii and The Sotavento
Speed Championships in Fuerteventura, Canary Islands. His
first book "An Introduction to Windsurfing" was published in
1987. *Boards* magazine has described him as "Britain's most
frequently photographed and most radical wavesailor".

The principal photographer
Alex Williams is one of Europe's most prolific watersports
photographers. Having come from a surfing background, he
became involved in windsurfing's embryonic funboard stages
in 1980. He is perhaps best known for his work within the water
– swimming around in somewhat challenging conditions to
capture the action at close quarters. Breaking manoeuvres
down into step-by-step photographs, using an 800mm lens, is
another of his strong points. Alex's work can be frequently
seen in the world's windsurfing press across all five continents.

The illustrator
Simon Evans studied illustration and design at Cornwall
College, qualifying in 1983. He started surfing in 1979 and took
up windsurfing five years later. He has windsurfed in Australia
and the west coast of France; most of his windsurfing has
taken place near his home in Cornwall at beaches such as
Hayle Rivermouth, Gwithian and Marazion. Simon now lives in
Falmouth, Cornwall, where he has an illustration and design
studio. A number of his clients are directly involved in the
surfing and windsurfing industry. He has also illustrated
another book in this Adventure Sports series – "Surfing"
(Salamander Books Ltd.) Simon still takes every opportunity to
surf or windsurf whenever the waves or wind allow.

CONTENTS

INTRODUCTION

I recall quite vividly my initiation into the windsurfing scene, way back in the dim and distant past. The spark that started the flame was struck by an old friend, Bernie Pugh. Bernie, an entrepreneur and professor in the "university of life", had acquired a couple of most unusual objects while on vacation in St. Tropez in southern France.

I had done a spot of dinghy sailing while at school, however, with mixed emotions. Every Wednesday in the Spring and Summer terms, we would go to the local sailing club for an afternoon of tuition in elementary sailing skills. Everything in school time, as you can imagine, had to be done by the book. A special sequence for rigging up, a log book and report and, somewhere in between the red tape, we might have slipped in ten minutes of sailing in the three-hour ordeal. It wasn't my idea of fun, although on breezier days (Force 3–4) we really felt like we had reached the limit. From a constructive angle, a basic knowledge of the theory of sailing was grasped – in hindsight, a blessing in disguise!

So, off I went with good old Bernie and these two objects lashed precariously to the roof of the car with reams of baling twine. We set off towards a destination in North Wales – Lake Bala. The drive lasted nearly four hours; at the time it seemed more like going on holiday than a day trip. Throughout the journey the boards swayed around on the roofrack in the breeze – a kind of acceptable ritual, I suppose.

On arrival we found we were not alone; another four people had similar craft and were already out on, or should I say, in the water. I knew the preparation would be a long process, having learnt this from my sailing experience. I must admit it took a while to put the jigsaw of pieces together even though I had someone to copy. However, it was easy donning a wetsuit that was two sizes too large, and it felt warm as toast never having worn one previously.

The sailing itself was a task to behold. Instruction was at a bare minimum, which didn't help the proceedings one little bit! Indeed, it took another six months of recreational sailing before we even began to steer in a predetermined direction. However, we were not the only ones – it took months for every sailor to emulate anything glimpsed at in a rare magazine publication. Since those early days, when other board-sailors were a scarce sight even during vacations, the sport has developed into a mature state. Particularly in Europe, boardsailing rapidly grew out of all expected proportion. In France you could pick up a board with your shopping in the local supermarket. Consequently the French flocked to the seas by the thousands.

The Europeans did not respond quite so quickly as the Americans to the funboard revolution. The introduction of shorter, more manoeuvrable models transformed the face of the sport to the extent that, today we see dynamic state-of-the-art equipment scattered in every sandy cove! Correspondingly the options for the riders themselves are infinite. A host of both simple and complex ways of changing direction, riding waves, racing and, most spectacularly, jumping clean out of the water has evolved in direct correlation to the equipment progression.

In winds too excessive for the competence of many in the yachting fraternity, the advancing windsurfer can display quite comfortably a vast array of entertaining skills. Slowly but surely the public at large is getting some insight into the sport as it exists today, as opposed to the once ubiquitous image of a holiday-maker trying to haul up an old rag of a sail at the seaside.

Of course, with all high-profile sports such as hang-gliding, surfing, mountain biking and white water kayaking there is an in-built element of danger. Remember the strongest man on earth is no match for the power of the sea. Use this force wisely, like the old fisherman, and turn it to your own advantage. The remainder of any risk is then purely down to yourself and how far your conscience will allow you to push the limits. With a modicum of common sense, no aspiring adventurer should come to any grief.

There has never been an easier time in which to sharpen windsurfing skills. Technique books, videos and magazines can offer an insight into something that could take months to perfect by pure trial and error. Windsurfing schools for advanced courses in improving old techniques and introducing new ones are a real asset.

So good luck and happy windskimming!

CHAPTER 1

PIONEERS TO THE PRESENT

Windsurfing in its short but eventful existence has probably grown in size and stature more rapidly than any other sport in history. Unlike many sports windsurfing has developed a real cosmopolitan flavour, with no geographical limits to its popularity. It has been accepted on the shores of all the great oceans of the world, and on inland waters as well.

Windsurfing's increasingly high profile attracted both young and old alike, and in France in particular it took off as a family sport, a sport for all, regardless of age. Worldwide there are now reckoned to be 15 million participants. It appears that there is no limit to the sport's potential expansion.

THE FUNBOARD REVOLUTION

The year 1977 saw something of a milestone in sailboard technology, with an invention that was to change the face of the sport. Along with many others, two Hawaiian sailors, Horgan and Stanley, had experienced the difficulties of sailing in high winds and rough surf. In these conditions the board became increasingly hard to control as the wind picked up, and often resulted in a dramatic catapult fall over the nose of the board. In surf and good wind the more capable sailors found that they could get the board airborne off wavelets. However, staying on for the landing was not always guaranteed! To make mat-

ters easier Horgan and Stanley came up with the simple but ingenious solution of the footstrap which kept the sailor's feet firmly in contact with the board in difficult conditions. But even with footstraps and without a full daggerboard the stock Windsurfer was still rather large and cumbersome in the surf. The Kailua Kids (early performers who virtually all came from Kailua on the Hawaiian island of Oahu) came up with the solution that seems in hindsight so obvious, namely making the board shorter without a dagger at all. After careful market study Hoyle Schweitzer, a Californian entrepreneur, produced a short jump board known as the windsurfer "Rocket", and soon

kids were jumping for joy in their Hawaiian playground!

For a couple of years jump style boards remained pretty similar to the Rocket, having excessively wide tails to facilitate maximum lift off the waves. These shortboards were still by today's standards pretty large, incorporating plenty of volume for that all-important quick uphaul or tack between the waves. In winds of Force 4 and beyond, higher performance and custom models could easily breeze along in excess of 15 knots and high speed gybing became a real art. The old style flare gybe became redundant when it became clear that funboards could be banked around their turn rather like a water skier cutting an arc. This "carve" gybe remains a standard manoeuvre in good shortboard technique.

Right: More recent portraits of The Kailua Kids – (from top to bottom) Matt Schweitzer, Mike Waltze and Robby Naish. Today, they are all still actively involved at the top end of high-performance shortboarding. Naish travels around performing in wave, course and slalom disciplines. Schweitzer and Waltze are now Maui residents.

Below: On a good day at the popular site of Hookipa in Maui, it's easy to see 100 sails plus!

THE NEXT GENERATION

In 1980 another vital manoeuvre in the funboard repertoire, the deep waterstart, was developed. Introduced originally as a trick, it quickly superseded the sometimes difficult and tiring ritual of uphauling in the surf and higher winds. Prior to this a beach launch or uphaul had been the only way of getting aboard.

Mike Waltze, one of the Kailua Kids, sailing on the Hawaiian island of Maui, soon cottoned on to other openings made possible by the waterstart. After converting a surfboard, he found he could sail smaller boards than had hitherto seemed possible, provided there was sufficient wind.

Together with Sailboards Maui, Waltze began to develop progressively smaller surfboard oriented designs, eventually getting to a point where the board had so little flotation (volume) that it would not support the sailor's own weight when not in motion. These extremely manoeuvrable "sinkers", as they became known, were waterstartable only. Their light weight also made them an asset while jumping, and the increased directional control gave Waltze the scope to sail bigger and better wave venues. At the now world-famous Hookipa Beach Park on the Hawaiian island of Maui, he could actually ride the wave in a style akin to surfing.

SAILS TALK

While Waltze was out battling at Hookipa, local sailmakers Spanier and Bourne (Maui Sails) took a keen interest in his exploits, and saw an immediate need for a specialized surf-sail, special both in terms of strength and improved handling. First generation surf-sails with their foot area and long boom – typically 8½ft (2.65m) – had a habit of catching in the water. Sail designers responded fast with a new concept of a high aspect ratio sail, tall and narrow in appearance. As the boom was shortened, the mast length was increased, resulting in a more rectangular shaped sail. In order to minimize the risk of involuntary contact with the water, the clew of the sail was elevated. The high-clew surf-sail quickly became an indispensible item of equipment.

It was some time before the benefits of these new developments began to take effect in European waters, since shortboard sailing still remained an almost exclusively Hawaiian preoccupation. Then in late 1981, German-born F2 star Jürgen Honscheid travelled from Hawaii to participate in the Weymouth Speed Trials in Britain. With him came the latest revolutionary sails and a sinker-style board – basically a surfboard he picked up and converted on the way. The public and media alike were amazed at the results – the board was extremely manoeuvrable, and Honscheid's carve gybing technique outstanding. For good measure Jürgen broke the windsurfing speed record, but not by the extra two per cent required to get it into the record books.

The 1983–84 season saw an expansion of the windsurfing-related industry, a great increase in numbers of participants, and another craze from Hawaiian waters – the "duck" gybe. Pioneers like Oahu's Richard Whyte could "duck" under the boom in mid gybe: the effect was similar to that of the carve gybe, but more stylish. The latest short-boom high-clew sails were a real asset to this transition, allowing easy passage for the sailor to travel

under the rig. Some sailors even had handles sewn on the foot of the sail, an aid for passing it over the head – but this gimmick did not catch on.

Suddenly sail development took another unexpected tangent. Existing sails in the higher "short-board" winds would distort badly, resulting in all kinds of handling problems for the sailor. In an effort to reduce this problem of distortion, the performance of rigs in other fields of sailing was studied, notably that of high-performance catamarans. Full length battens were introduced into windsurfer sails, resulting in a much cleaner foil shape, which increased sail stability; the cause of previous handling problems, shifting of the centre of effort, was overcome by the use of rigid battens.

Almost overnight the whole windsurfing scene became very fashion-conscious. If the sailor didn't have a battened sail that resembled the rungs of a ladder, he felt decidedly underdressed for the occasion.

These fully battened rigs, some incorporating new Mylar cloths, were far more sophisticated than their immediate forebears. The sail when combined with a stiff mast, necessary for the long luff length, was not only easier to control, but also more efficient. As a direct result of technological advance, the speed record was steadily pushed up in the following months. Taking this "hard" set sail to the extreme, Britain's Fred Haywood became the first man to crash through the 30-knot barrier, creating an achievement almost unthinkable only a few years before.

Left: Waterstarts, now regarded as a basic move, transformed the realms of surf-sailing and high wind – a new era was born.

Above: Early surf-sails had a high clew yet still retained a long boom and no foot batten.

Right: Jürgen Honscheid, in retirement from competition, is seen here sailing offshore of his now native island of Fuerteventura in the Canaries.

THE OLYMPICS

With the sport still less than 20 years old, and hence in its infancy, windsurfing became the youngest sport ever to attain Olympic status, marking an important moment in the history of the sport. Windsurfing had finally received the recognition it deserved. The 1984 games in Los Angeles incorporated triangle racing on flatboards. The chosen board for this yacht-type course was the Ostermann Windglider. Although the Windglider was already a bit old-fashioned, it was not as daunting as having to sail the long course without the use of a harness which was not permitted in the games of that year.

AERIAL ANTICS

While many windsurfers travelled world-wide in search of racing victories, others at the opposite end of the funboard spectrum felt impelled to take up the challenge of bigger surf. For them wavejumping was the name of the game, and the development of high-tech sails led to increasingly spectacular jumps.

Kicks were the norm, but it was not long before a rotating movement of board, rig and sailor was discovered. This barrel roll or loop involved jumping up and taking the nose of the board into and through the eye of the wind. Landings were few and far between for the early loopers like France's Raphael Salles and Maui's Doug Hunt, and indeed life and limb were also at great risk while attempting this very difficult manoeuvre.

EQUIPMENT PROGRESSION

The world's more progressive sail lofts (retail outlets) had exploited the full-batten concept to the extreme, though perhaps the most significant change in rig design was just around the corner. The continual development process arrived at a batten below the boom, or footbatten, which gave the sail a vast increase in efficiency. For wavesailing it was no longer an absolute necessity to have a collection of full length battens. An option

Above: Hawaiian Peter Cabrinha gracefully demonstrates the old style windward loop or barrel roll as it is otherwise known.

Below: A modern fully-battened sail being put through its paces. These battens extend all the way to the mast.

had evolved where the footbatten gave the sail enough stability to work just as well in a soft mode (short leech battens) as it had previously in a hard one (full battens).

For slalom, course and speed sailing a hard set sail was still the order of the day. To harden up the sails still further, all battens sat against the mast and flicked around it when changing tack. All forms of racing relied on either this rotating asymmetric foil (RAF) system, or another efficient concept, the camber-inducer. This tuning-fork type of mechanism straddled the mast, inducing a hard leading edge and following profile into the contour of the sail.

The camber system forcefully struck windsurfers' attention when, in 1986 at the Sotavento Speed Week in Fuerteventura (Canary Islands), Frenchman Pascal Maka achieved an amazing 38 knots, surpassing the old record by a six-knot margin. Maka's sail, incorporating six inducers and eight battens, worked in winds approaching 40 knots without undue distortion. This high-tech sail, in conjunction with a selection of custom-made "speed-needle" boards, proved a very effective combination.

Mass-produced boards, though by now excellent in both construction and performance, were no longer any match for their custom cousins. In all aspects of the sport, one could find a custom design suited to both the sailor and the conditions that prevailed. Although production boards were adequate for general high wind sailing, for the more serious business of competitive surf, speed and slalom sailing, a selection of custom-made boards and a compatible quiver of rigs was the order of the day.

THE DANGER ELEMENT

Dangers to life and limb grew in direct proportion to increases in performance. The hazards of high jumps in big waves are readily apparent but, in addition to these, recently developed manoeuvres have added their share of danger. Notable among the latter is the forward roll, conceived by the Italian Cesare Cantagalli. Here, instead of looping into the wind – as in the barrel roll – the sailor attempts a downwind corkscrew-like motion, if he makes a mistake in mid-loop he is liable to drop like a stone onto his own equipment, sometimes from a great height. Prudent windsurfers have taken to wearing crash hats as broken noses and various other head injuries have disfigured the appearance of the fraternity!

THE CURRENT SCENE

Today windsurfing is far removed from the "good old days" of the original Windsurfer. Even in his wildest dreams Hoyle Schweitzer could hardly have anticipated the extent to which the sport caught on world-wide.

Hawaii, or more specifically Maui, remains the research and development centre for major manufacturers. Many of the top professionals are either bred or trained around its shores. Yet by far the largest number of participants are based in Europe, predominantly in France, Germany and Great Britain.

Equipment is becoming increasingly uniform world-wide as the pace of innovation slows down. Changes are now largely of a slight, or cosmetic, character. Hybrid materials play a significant role in the sport, giving strength and weight benefits for all, whether racing or just sailing for fun.

Never has there been a better time to learn, or to improve. Instructional media, practical courses and improved equipment all play a part in raising standards. To breeze around a course, pull a full forward loop or even join the likes of Britain's Eric Beale into the 40-knots club all might have seemed a remote possibility at one time; now these possibilities are within the grasp of many.

Left: Crash hats can frequently be seen on both the hair-raising speed course and in challenging wave conditions.

Below: Waveboards are by far the most comfortable boards to hop around on, yet with good technique, a large slalomboard can be pushed to the limit.

CHAPTER 2

THE VITAL COMPONENTS

All boards available today are either production or custom made. Production models are made in large numbers using a moulding process. Each unit is therefore identical to all the others in the batch, and will perform in the same manner. Since tooling up for the moulding process can be cost-intensive, larger manufacturers tend to change design on a yearly basis, hoping that the numbers produced will spread the initial fixed cost.

Custom boards are shaped from a foam blank, one at a time, and then hand laminated in a skilled and time-consuming process. However, each board can be individually tuned to suit particular conditions or a sailor's own idiosyncracies. In terms of performance, custom boards are generally superior to production boards; they certainly dominate the arenas of wave and speedsailing and indeed, the upper echelons of funboard racing.

PERFORMANCE BOARDS

Construction

The material used in construction is often worth investigating. Boards at the mass end of the market are often made from plastic derivatives such as polyethylene and the better finished ABS (a popular plastic material amongst board manufacturers). These plastics, although relatively cheap to produce and ideal for recreational use, offer little in terms of high performance. Fibreglass, in general, is both lighter and stiffer than any of the plastics and although structurally stronger is, at the same time, less resistant to damage. There are two resin types used in conjunction with the fibreglass and these are polyester and epoxy. Epoxy resins are best suited to hybrid materials incorporating carbon and kevlar, resulting in a

Right: A custom and production slalomboard, with very similar dimensions, are seen here.

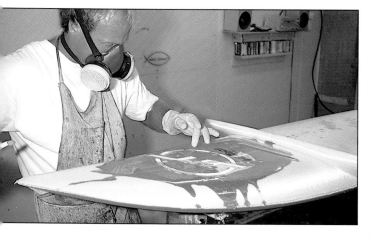

Above: Hand laminating a custom board is a highly skilful and time-consuming process.

Below: A waveboard's banana-like rocker makes it very responsive in critical situations.

very light and stiff board. Epoxy, while being more ding resistant than polyester, is more difficult to work with and carries a hefty price tag. Polyester resins are most popular in custom board manufacture, where its ease of work and quick setting times are an obvious advantage.

Over the last couple of years board design has stabilized into specific categories – no longer do new boards of radical design appear and eclipse existing models. Understanding of the important variables has increased to a point where a slight change in one variable can be almost isolated in its effect on performance.

The most important of the design parameters is the board's rocker line. Rocker is the amount of curvature from nose to tail and this is what dictates how quickly the board will plane, and its turning circle. The tail rocker is the more critical for performance. A small rocker allows quick acceleration and top speed. As the tail rocker increases, speed is reduced while the board's manoeuvrability increases. As a result raceboards tend to have only a slight rocker whereas waveboards, with a need for rapid directional change, require more tail rocker. Additionally, they also need more nose rocker to prevent the board nose diving when dropping down a waveface.

The board's edges or rails are also critical to its behaviour and performance and can be either hard or soft in section. A hard rail gives good water release allowing the board to plane early, and a trade-off exists between this water release and the board's grip in the water. The harder the rail, the better the pick up, yet during turns a hard rail tends to trip. For the aspiring course and slalom sailor a hard rail is a must, even if it means extra concentration during gybes.

Soft rails have completely the opposite effect, while although slow, they will harbour water making the board grip during even the tightest turns. For wavesailing a soft rail is essential in order to execute reasonable turns on the wave itself. Often the rail will harden up a touch towards the tail to achieve some sort of early planing.

A board's outline shape can be divided into three regions – nose width, tail width and wide point. The last has the greatest effect on the board's manoeuvrability. The wide point can be back, central, or forward. The more forward it is, the greater the directional stability – the further back, the greater the manoeuvrability. The actual tail width is probably more important than the shape of the tail itself; a wide tail facilitates early planing and gives great lift for jumps, while a narrow tail controls better in high winds, but necessitates long drawn out turns. The nose width is the least important outline variant. A wide nose will aid early planing and give the board extra stability in light airs, while in stronger airs, particularly if it's choppy, the wide nose can catch and disrupt the board's equilibrium.

A board's volume will dictate how it will lie in the water. Volume is measured in litres, and one litre of volume will float a one kilogram mass. It does not follow that an 80 litre board will support an 80 litre sailor when stationary, since the weight of the rig has to be taken into account. Equally important is the relative distribution of volume within the length of the board. Most boards have maximum volume about the mast track, where the sailor's effective weight is transferred into a pushing movement, via the rig. A little volume in the front of the board can be an asset when it comes to tacking. However, a voluminous tail, although keeping the board level, can be detrimental in strong airs as immense weight and pressure will be needed to make the board turn.

The final design parameter to consider is the hull's hydrodynamic characteristics, or its underwater shape. In recent years, concaves, channels and scoops (curvatures of the nose) have all been in and out of vogue more often than miniskirts, it would seem. The object of these underwater configurations is to get air under the board to create lift. Concaves are at their extreme in raceboards, where early light wind planing is essential. In more subtle forms slalom and speedboards utilize the concave theory. However, too much induced air can cause handling problems in severe winds.

The tail section of most boards incorporates a "V" shaped profile in its design to give added directional stability. A more pronounced "V", as in waveboards, aids better rail-to-rail transitions and, once again, a sweeter turn.

Below: This slalomboard shows a fascinating combination of early planing concaves.

Types of boards

In the classification of boards, length is the normal yardstick, though for our purposes it is perhaps better to categorize boards in terms of their specific use, for example, course racer or waveboard. A typical course racing board, whether production or custom (the latter being less common) is between 12 and 12½ft (3.6 and 3.8m) in length. Its rails are its most distinctive feature, being of a box section, running right through in order to gain early planing and upwind performance. The deck features include numerous footstraps – the back ones for reaching and the front ones for beating. A fully retracting daggerboard is pos-

TYPES OF BOARDS

Courseboard

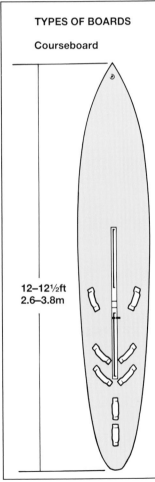

12–12½ft
2.6–3.8m

itioned centrally and is fully down for the upwind work and fully retracted for off the wind reaches. Double or quadruple concaves feature prominently on the underside and are especially pronounced in the nose section. The lighter the board, the better for that all important acceleration at the start and out of the turns.

Slalomboards range from 8½ to 10ft (2.6 to 3.0m) in length depending on the wind strength they are designed for – the stronger the wind, the shorter the board. Again, hard rails are in evidence, combined with a very small rocker. Footstrap configurations do vary slightly; normally there is one set of front straps with a single or double

rear set, the rearmost being some 12ins (3cm) in length from the tail. Lighter wind models feature stronger concaves, as early planing and high top end speed are the main priorities here.

Waveboards vary more than most other types of board in terms of design. They are often built with the prevailing conditions in mind, and a slight change in one of the design parameters can radically change performance. Tail and nose rocker are normally extensive – up to 2ins (7cm) in some waveboard tails. Soft rails feature prominently in the front two-thirds of the boards which rarely exceed 9ft (2.7m) in length. Smaller models have so little volume that they actually sink

under the sailor's weight when not in motion.

Perhaps the strangest phenomenon in board design is the asymmetrical waveboard, where one side of the board is designed for a smooth bottom turn, and the other for a snappy cut-back. Asymmetrics are in common use in locations where the wind blows consistently cross-shore from one direction, otherwise a board for each tack is normally required.

The last and certainly the most eye-catching board is the speed-needle. Purely designed for speed off the wind, a speedboard can range from a light wind 18ins (46cm) wide to a world record attempting 10½ins (27cm) wide.

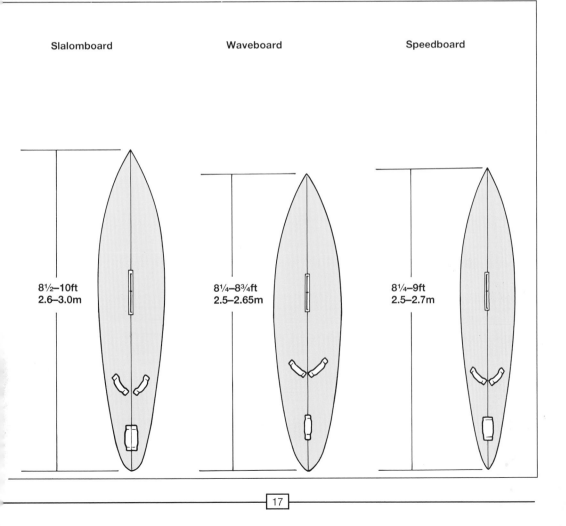

Slalomboard

Waveboard

Speedboard

8½–10ft
2.6–3.0m

8¼–8¾ft
2.5–2.65m

8¼–9ft
2.5–2.7m

Only a few manufacturers produce production speedsters and those are mainly for lighter winds – below 30 knots in terms of wind speed. The faster boards not only have narrow length overall, but taper down to even narrower tails. Contemporary shapes feature a single concave hull, often with chined rails which is theoretically the most efficient shape. The smaller boards are of little use unless the wind is very strong and the water flat. They can therefore be regarded as an exotic but necessary item in the speedsailor's quiver.

For world record attempts, the narrower boards really come into their own, especially on the ultra smooth man-made courses.

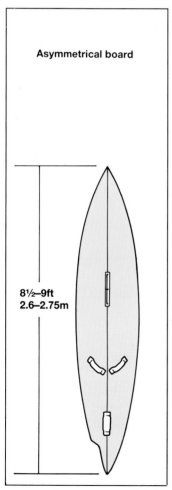

Asymmetrical board

8½–9ft
2.6–2.75m

PERFORMANCE SAILS

There is more to a modern windsurfing sail than meets the eye. Sail design has modified the nature of the once ubiquitous triangular rag into a highly specialized product. As in board construction, there are a number of variables which dictate how a sail will perform, and consequently which type of sailing it will be most suited to.

The most important considerations are outline shape and fullness. The first is related to mast bend or luff curve and the ratio of boom length to mast length (aspect ratio). Sails built for speed tend to have less luff curve than say a wavesail. A straight luff is in principle more efficient, yet not as manoeuvrable as would be a sail with increased luff curve, as applied to wavesails. The aspect ratio of a sail relates to whether it is short and squat as in

course racing, or tall and thin as in speedsailing. An infinite series of shapes exists between the two incorporating recreational and wavesails – see diagram.

The final outline shape of the sail is dictated by the sail's roach, which is the additional area lying outside the triangle, linking head, clew and tack. This unsupported part of the sail has to be propped up by battens. Generally speaking, sails for lighter airs have more leech roach than stronger wind designs which help the sail to gather wind. The roach at the upper area of the leech is also responsible for twist – a little twist is a desirable thing, helping the sail spill wind by opening the leech. Too much twist caused by too fat a head, however, will tend to lead to rig distortion giving adverse handling. The classic example of inbuilt twist is the cutaway sail. Unfortunately it works better in theory than in practice!

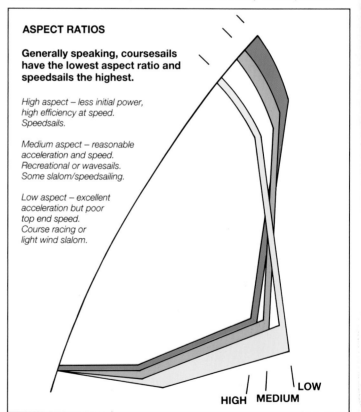

ASPECT RATIOS

Generally speaking, coursesails have the lowest aspect ratio and speedsails the highest.

High aspect – less initial power, high efficiency at speed. Speedsails.

Medium aspect – reasonable acceleration and speed. Recreational or wavesails. Some slalom/speedsailing.

Low aspect – excellent acceleration but poor top end speed. Course racing or light wind slalom.

LOW

HIGH MEDIUM

The foot roach of the sail influences its efficiency. Sails which adapt to racing have a large foot roach to gain an early closing of the gap between board and rig. As soon as this "slot" is shut, turbulence under the sail is reduced. A speedsail illustrates the ultimate in foot roach – the rig is hardly raked back yet the slot is closed.

The point of maximum fullness is termed the draught of the sail, and the relative position and depth of the draught should correspond to the sail's proposed use. High wind sails incorporate a flatter forward draught (27 to 30 per cent) resulting in control at the apex while planing, but with poor acceleration. For lighter airs a full further back draught (35 to 40 per cent) will create immense lift which, for course racing, is ideal. As the wind increases the sail should be set a little flatter, or less full, otherwise its drag to lift ratio will increase. Obviously outline and fullness are not separate entities. They naturally cohabit in a fixed form so that the sail can do its appropriate work.

Right: The cutaway sail gave the impression that the large head would twist off and aid control.

Below left: A typical course racing sail with the usual excess of roach at the foot and along the leech or trailing edge.

Below: Speedsails hold the most foot roach of all, making it a lot easier to close the slot. This was carried out by raking the rig back just a fraction.

Types of sails

For practical purposes sails fall into one of two categories – hard and soft foils. The camber-induced sail is at the extreme of the "hard set" spectrum. The batten forces the inducer against the mast, giving a hard leading edge and consequent clean air flow.

Induced sails, with their superb leeward and windward airflow, are very efficient and stable. For serious course racers, be it slalom or speed, they are a must. Even so, it has to be said that the quality and positioning of inducers is variable. A speedsail can carry up to seven inducers within a total of nine battens. Gybing with such a sail is not particularly comfortable, especially when all cambers flick from tack to tack. This is why course and slalom rigs tend to limit themselves to two to four inducers to give the sail a little more all-round scope. Racing apart, induced rigs are not as user-friendly as other types of sails. The wide luff tends to fill with water after a wipe-out, and the fixed profile cradles water, making uphauling and waterstarting difficult.

The rotating asymmetric foil, or RAF as it is more commonly known, also falls into the "hard" sail category. Here the full length battens lie adjacent to the mast giving a clean and stable air flow. When changing tack, the battens will rotate or flick about the mast to establish the required foil shape on the other side. Provided that the rig is set correctly (i.e. rotates easily) the RAF will be very stable in strong airs. RAF sails are used in recreational sailing, wavesailing and, in some instances, speedsailing. It is therefore not surprising to discover that the RAF is the most commonly used sail in windsurfing.

The term "soft" denotes any sail which has half battens as opposed to full length battens in its leech section. Other than handling, there may be very little difference between it and its RAF counterpart. The beauty of an unsupported luff panel is that it can be depowered and repowered in a split second. At critical moments the sail can suddenly be made windless, giving the rider that all-important extra mo-

ment to react – the margin for error is usefully extended.

In wavesailing, where the soft sail competes with similar RAF's, it becomes apparent that in very strong winds the first is not as stable as the last. The choice of a softer sail in these circumstances is normally a matter of personal preference.

In an effort to get the best of both worlds many wave type sails are made with a dual batten system, (DBS) which allows for both facilities i.e. short or full length battens. This system gives good scope for recreational sailors who have to manage with both wave and flat water sailing.

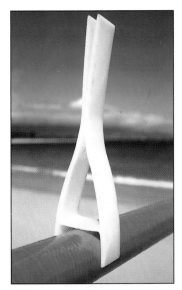

Right: This camber-inducer has been removed from the luff tube of a course racing sail.

Above: The RAF is a very stable sail – popular for jumping.

Below: Dual batten system sails use short or long battens.

MASTS

Most users give their masts very little thought. Besides varying in diameter, length and colour, they may differ in other important ways.

The internal base diameter of masts is more or less universal. Two sizes predominate: the narrower 1¾ins (4.6cm) is a survival from the old days, being the exact diameter of the original Windsurfer mast, while the commoner 2ins (4.85cm) mast is the standard gauge of the large European board manufacturers. The most common mast length is 15¼ft (4.65m). Most modern sails have floating heads to accommodate any length mast. An adjustable extension will compensate for short masts or even long luff lengths.

The technical attributes of material, stiffness and bend curve are all matters of interest to the practising sailor. Masts are made from either fibreglass or aluminium – the first for waves, the last for racing. Fibreglass masts are generally stronger than aluminium and can take the sudden loading of a breaking wave in their stride. Under similar stress the aluminium may kink or shear in two. Fibreglass masts, although strong, are by no means indestructible since many sailors in big surf over shallow water have found this to their cost.

Modern masts are much stiffer than the bendy poles of old. Moreover, modern sails are designed to set on these stiff masts. Racing sails, with their reduced luff curve, are set best on very stiff masts. These masts tend to be aluminium which has inherent weight-saving advantages for the racer. Often a sailmaker will recommend a mast for the cut of the sail.

As a general rule, if vertical creases appear in the luff area, the mast is not stiff enough.

Right: This set of masts, from left to right, includes a fibreglass wave mast, a two-piece mast and an aluminium race mast. It's important to correlate the correct mast to its respective type of sail for better fun and function.

BOOMS

Today's sailor carries a wider range of sizes and shapes of sail than ever before. Most booms are adjustable in length, so that one boom alone can accommodate three or four separate sails. Booms may be adjusted in one of two ways – by adding on extension tubes or by a telescopic action. The add-on variety is lighter in use; however, other length tubes are forever kicking around or getting lost on dry land. If the extension tubes are left unaltered for a time they can corrode up or jam with sand, and if you are unlucky the damage may be permanent. Telescopic booms adjust in finer increments, usually 2ins (5cm) intervals, so that the boom end is never far away from the sail. The drawback with telescopics is that they do require some maintenance. Prevention is the best medicine here; a fresh-water rinse from time to time will keep your boom clean and lengthen its life.

A boom's front end merits some consideration. There has to be a tight connection to the mast. The clamp or ski binding approach is certainly the simplest, but it has to be said that there are good and bad clamp systems.

The physical strength of the boom is of paramount concern to the high wind sailor, which de-

Below: Two booms of similar use, yet one is telescopic and the other has add-on sections.

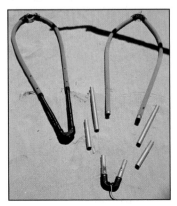

pends largely on the ends and on the quality of the tubing. An excessively flexible boom is probably a weak one. Avoid using any boom for long periods on its maximum extension as this is when it is most susceptible to breakage. Boom failures, especially in surf, can lead to lots of other equipment damage.

The grip is an item of practical as well as cosmetic value. Try to use a boom with a user-friendly finish such as Progrip. Grips in tougher materials may last longer but won't do your hands a lot of good.

Below: One of the most popular and reliable clamp boom ends.

FINS

Modern fins are available in a variety of styles. Normally they are made to do a specific job whether it be a 7½ins (19cm) speed fin or a 13ins (33cm) course racing fin. Always match up the fin to its respective type of board.

The basic things to remember about fins are that an upright fin is fast and a swept back fin is manoeuvrable. Upright fins, of varying depths, are therefore appropriate for racing and swept back fins are used more for recreational and wavesailing.

There are, of course, good and bad examples of fins. The construction and foil shape play an important role here. Better fins tend to be handmade in fibreglass, although some glass-filled moulded fins are acceptable. A good fin is always stiff along its length.

The bugbear of all performance windsurfers is spin-out. Spin-out – or cavitation – occurs when the fin gets over aerated and as a result

loses its grip, making the board almost impossible to control. Spin-out is due either to a bad fin or to defective control. To retrieve the situation, sheet out and release pressure on the tail of the board.

A relatively recent development in fin technology is the window or slot-effect. This slot, parallel and towards the leading edge, has proved to be another useful way to combat spin-out. These window fins are used occasionally in slalomsailing, but primarily in wave or shortboards, where the extreme pressures of jumping are experienced. The increased drag of the slot gives the fin little application in course and speedsailing.

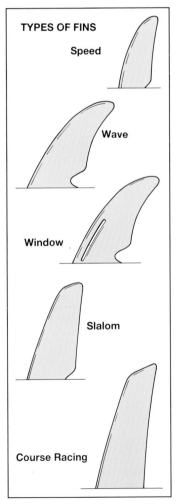

TYPES OF FINS

Speed

Wave

Window

Slalom

Course Racing

FOOTSTRAPS

Without the humble footstrap, windsurfing would not be the exciting sport we know. The strap itself consists of inner webbing, which takes the strain, and an outer neoprene cover to comfort the rider's foot – also to gladden his eye! The strap is adjustable in length to suit most feet sizes by Velcro closures situated beneath the outer cover. The strap itself is resined into the deck or screwed into preinserted mountings. The last method is most widely adopted as it allows for the possibility of easy strap removal should that be deemed necessary.

Above: A top quality footstrap is only safe and comfortable if it fits snug over the foot.

WETSUITS

In virtually all climates a wetsuit of some description is a necessity. The garment can take many forms, whether a thin vest or a thick all-in-one affair. The style of suit will depend on the prevailing conditions.

The criteria that control the warmth of a suit are thickness, fitting, material and construction method. For maximum warmth a suit should be a close fit; however, it should not fit too well in the forearm and bicep area, as these tend to expand while sailing.

Thick suits of 4 and 5mm are for colder climes and conditions and are usually full length in both arms and legs. For the die-hard arctic windsurfer a dry suit is an alternative, even though in practice they are a mite cumbersome, fragile and expensive. Thinner suits of 2 and 3mm are for warmer climates. The summer suits range from neoprene vests, shorts, shorties, long johns and short/long arm full suits.

Most sailors are well aware of the dangers of hypothermia, which is brought on by insufficient insulation leading to a plummet of the body's core temperature. In hotter latitudes one has to be on the look out for hyperthermia, or dehydration, caused by wearing too warm a suit.

Here are listed some tips for preserving you wetsuit and extending its useful life:
☐ Before long storage be sure to rinse it out in fresh water and hang it up to prevent creasing
☐ Do not lend your suit to another person if you can help it – your suit's adaptation to your unique body contours could well be irreversibly lost
☐ Fit the suit as you roll it on upwards; this will prevent undue stress on the seams
☐ Always hold the base of the zip before pulling it up, as suits are very prone to damage in this area

Left: Summer style wetsuits can take any one of these distinct forms. The final choice really depends on the temperature of both water and air.

COLD WEATHER KITS

Provided that the appropriate protection is worn, windsurfing can still be enjoyed in very cold conditions, where the wind-chill factor may push down temperatures that are already low. A good pair of neoprene boots is a must and should be a snug fit to maintain the heat.

As the temperature drops below the 12°C barrier, further protective measures are called for. The greatest bodily heat loss is through the head, so a hat or hood is an absolute necessity. Gloves, even less popular than hats, are also indispensable in extreme conditions despite the fact that they reduce the sailor's sensitivity to the rig (and to the wind).

HARNESSES

The object of the harness and harness lines is to relieve the pull of the rig from the sailor's arms. The rider's body weight is thus allowed to counterbalance the rig, permitting the sailor to be on the water for much longer.

With some minor modifications harnesses take three main forms, focusing on waist, chest and seat. The waist harness is most popular with wave and recreational sailors as it offers the best freedom of movement. Back support and personal buoyancy is at a minimum – the last being a point to bear in mind. For better support and leverage, some waist harnesses offer a "bum-strap" attachment.

The more traditional chest harness offers better support for the often susceptible lower back region. Sometimes, when jumping and particularly when attempting loops, it is common to land flat on the back; in these circumstances full back coverage can cushion a potentially stinging blow.

Seat-type harnesses are becoming increasingly popular. For course and slalom racing the lower hook enables increased purchase on the rig, and the virtual sitting down position of the seat forces the sailor into a correct body position. Some sailors prefer the seat harness for wavesailing.

Remember that lines, although set correctly last time you sailed, may not be properly set for, say, racing, or a change in sail size.

Top left: Winter or cold weather wetsuits don't have quite as much variation as their summer cousins. Virtually all these suits are one piece incorporating both long legs and arms. To keep water penetration to a minimum, the neoprene is both blind stitched and glued for good insulation – a "cup" stitch is used which leaves no holes.

Bottom left: This harness parade features the three principle styles of chest, seat and waist.

ARMOUR

Improvements in technology and performance can entail greater risks of personal injury. Many riders have taken to wearing crash helmets to minimize accidents affecting the head. Crash helmets are particularly favoured in speed events, where the danger of a high-speed catapult is greatest. There is also a good case for wearing such protection should you attempt a loop where there is a risk of landing on your own gear. A point worth considering here is the weight of the helmet – obviously the more lightweight the helmet, the less strain on the neck.

Specialist windsurfing armour – some of it reminiscent of American Football armour – is now available for the "go for it" windsurfer. Often a little cumbersome and inhibiting to free movement, it is nevertheless useful in certain learning situations. If nothing else, the sailor who wears this gear, full-face helmet and the rest, will certainly cut an impressive figure!

Just as there are measures to protect your health, there are measures to protect your wealth. Many useful accessories are available which will help keep your gear in good shape. On the water it is advisable to use a mast pad which will minimize damage from the extension during a wipe-out – this applies especially to custom boards. Scrupulous sailors use boom-buffers, which cover the front boom end to reduce damage should it be catapulted onto the deck of the board.

Damage is quite likely to occur off the water. Boards dropped off car roofs or dragged and blown along the ground are also a common occurrence – in these circumstances a board bag will minimize damage. In sunnier climates it will also protect the hull from harmful ultraviolet rays which can easily fade or discolour any graphics.

Below left: Specialist sailing body armour has evolved to offer protection and buoyancy.

Below: Board armour in the form of a padded bag is essential for all budding travellers.

CHAPTER 3

KEYS TO THE DOOR

Performance windsurfing offering high-profile action, along with the associated thrills and spills, is appealing to performers and spectators alike. "Performance" is an appropriate word, as an individual can develop a unique style of sailing, even his own peculiar idiosyncracies in the execution of certain manoeuvres. A high wind sailor does not necessarily have to get blown along with the pack – he can develop his own distinct style.

Whatever the individual's capacity, he still has his own "learning curve", and the sailor who can cope with gentle breezes still has to learn the more difficult art of high wind sailing. The key to successful learning is by proceeding in a methodical, step-by-step fashion – not trying to run before we can walk! But once the steps are mastered, the waters – be they lakes or the open sea, are there to be danced upon! The watchword is, therefore, "Look! Listen! Learn!"

RIGGING ANALYSIS

It is a cardinal, yet common, sin to hurry through the rigging-up process in the rush to get on the water. But time spent rigging correctly is not time wasted – on the contrary, it may save a lot of time wasting later on, in what may well be more difficult conditions.

The correct procedure is as follows: roll out the sail and slip the mast up the luff sleeve until the tip of the mast is securely in the head cap of the sail. Now apply a modicum of downhaul tension, just to keep the sail in place – if unfamiliar with the sail, stand the mast vertically to check for the correct boom height, this usually lies between chest and shoulder height. If the luff cut-out appears to be excessively high or low, examine the head region – it may incorporate an adjustable head, which should now be set before proceeding. Attach the boom at its correct height – be sure

the connection is firm and that the sail is not trapped in the boom's jaws. Outhaul and downhaul the sail; if the boom is the correct length the clew should not be far off the rear boom end. A mighty effort is often needed to downhaul most modern sails, and a foot on the mast foot will help proceedings. Finally insert and tension all battens. It's worth checking if they are split or broken as this occurs quite frequently in wavesails. Only fine-tuning is now needed.

Once fitted, the boom should be secure enough to stay horizontal without outhaul tension. For outhauling and downhauling, pulleys are almost essential, up to a 6:1 ratio for the latter. Pulling on the sheets (ropes) can easily burn your hands so, to prevent this and gain better grip, a tool or easy-rig is most useful. If the sail is camber-induced, make sure the inducers are in place before fully tensioning the battens, otherwise breakage

Above: The boom, when correctly positioned, should be between chest and shoulder height. A tight fit is essential.

Above: After a modicum of downhaul, outhaul the sail to its known boom length using pulleys or leverage if necessary.

Above: Fully downhaul the sail. For most modern sails, pulleys are essential – a foot on the mast base can help proceedings.

can occur. All that now remains is to fine-tune the outhaul and downhaul to suit the prevailing conditions. As the wind increases the sail should be set flatter by a combined effort of out and downhaul tension.

Derigging is a less complicated process since you basically reverse the rigging procedure. An important point is not to release outhaul tension while the downhaul is still taut. A soft set sail, normally with a Dacron luff panel, will stretch beyond recognition in no time at all.

Incorrect rigging

If the sail still looks wrong after being set, give special attention to the following possibilities:

☐ Lack of downhaul tension: this will cause the sail's draught to move violently fore and aft, making control of the sail very difficult. Horizontal lines across the sail or a lack of tension in the boom cut-out also indicate not enough downhaul.

☐ Lack of outhaul tension: the sail

will appear excessively full, perhaps touching the boom when sheeted in. Sailing in this mode, with the draught so far forward, can lead to endless catapults. On the other hand, never flatten the sail as it will appear powerless.

☐ Low batten tension: you will see wrinkles along the batten pockets; however it is quickly remedied, as long as the batten is not too short.

Although a sail may appear to be well set on being rigged, it may be a completely different story when you are on the water. After a few minutes in use you may note that lines have a tendency to creep in. Even prestretched rope will give a small amount in areas of high strain such as an adjustable head or downhaul. The answer is to keep your eyes open with regard to sail shape and performance; if anything untoward starts to occur, head straight back to the shore, where you will be able to carry out the necessary appropriate adjustments.

Above: Tension up the battens to finish off the rigging. Only then can fine trimming of out and downhaul take place.

Above: Insufficient batten tension is easily spotted and remedied. It is usually indicated by severe lines.

Top: Lack of downhaul, indicated by horizontal creases, is the most frequent rigging mistake making rig control difficult.

Wrong mast stiffness can be another problem. Although outhaul and downhaul may be exactly adjusted, a sloppy mast will cause vertical creases in the sail, particularly in the head region. For recreational sailing this is no big deal, yet for any form of racing it could seriously affect your chances.

If, after considering all the above aspects, the sail still sets badly, you may be forced to the conclusion that the sail is past its prime. Wavesails are particularly susceptible to premature ageing. In this case, pension it off, and get a new one.

Right: After a wipe-out, the rig can often fall into a tricky position. This makes it very difficult for the sailor to perform a waterstart.

WATERSTARTING

Waterstarting is an essential aspect of all progressive sailing. Shorter boards invariably require a waterstart, and indeed any sailor who has tried uphauling a larger board in stronger airs will readily appreciate the benefits of waterstarting. The style of board you are riding will dictate whether a waterstart or uphaul is appropriate. In the main, low volume boards, provided the wind is sufficient, are easier to waterstart every time. Once the technique is mastered it is advisable to use the waterstart on marginals and complete floaters since uphauling in rough seas can be tiring and difficult.

After a spill the rig and board are rarely in the ideal situation to waterstart immediately. You must therefore align the board across the wind (beam reach) and this can sometimes involve a swim – you may find on many occasions (this being a sort of maritime sod's law!) that the rig will be on the wrong side of the board and facing the wrong way. Get the rig into a position upwind of the board with the luff of the sail, as opposed to the clew, facing towards the wind. Holding the mast above the boom, draw the rig up and over the tail of the board – it should flap around freely after the

water has drained off. Using mast-foot pressure alone, steer the board slightly downwind, keeping the rig flying and staying close to the board (you should have both hands firmly on the boom). Put your front or rear foot (whichever seems most natural) into its respective footstrap. You can then – and only then – present the sail to the wind. To get aboard, simultaneously pump the rig and thrust your body in one movement out of the water. A broad reach position will create the most lift for this vital stage.

Often it can be difficult to raise the rig from the boom area. If the rig is well and truly stuck, then swim to the mast tip. While treading water, raise the mast tip into the wind. Slowly but surely the sail should start to release itself. As it releases, shin down the mast, hand over hand until just above the boom; at this point a start can be attempted.

As the wind gets progressively stronger, it may be necessary to present the sail with the board aligned a little closer to the wind, that is, not on a broad reach, otherwise the wind will not only pick you out of the water fast but fling you straight over the bows!

It is a good idea, until you become fluent, to practise the waterstart on a more buoyant board or in shallow waters. You can then be

both confident and safe in the knowledge that if you fail it will still be possible to return to terra firma without too much inconvenience.

Having mastered the technique of waterstarting, you will soon be wondering how you ever got along without it! It saves an awful lot of hassle, and may even save money for you in offering a quick exit from a potentially kit breaking situation – or even worse.

Top left: To effect a waterstart, get into position upwind and adjacent to the board. With one hand on the mast, keep the rig flying freely.

Top right: Raise the sail a little and place both hands on the boom in their normal place. Place one foot on board in anticipation of the lift.

Bottom left: To create the lift, gradually present the rig to the wind. As the pull increases, kick up and raise the rig further to climb aboard.

Bottom right: As soon as you are completely clear, settle down and trim the board so that it is level. Work the rig a touch to get onto the plane.

Light wind waterstarting

People are often seen venturing out on low volume boards in relatively light airs, which is not a good idea, since a fall in a Force 3 or less often results in a lengthy swim or unnecessary rescue. Sometimes, of course, it is just bad luck; the unfortunate sinker sailor finds himself out on a limb when the wind suddenly decides to die on him. Most often, though, it doesn't die without advanced warning.

Unless the wind vanishes completely, all is not lost, since with the correct technique, a light wind waterstart is possible. Flying the rig is initially much more difficult, as there is reduced aid from the wind itself. The sailor must tread water hard and even perhaps push up from a head-under-water position to unstick the rig. Once the rig is freed, by fair means or foul, it should be aligned with the board and across the wind in the usual manner. When both hands are securely in the sailing position, raise the sail slightly and drop the front hand onto the mast below the boom – this position, with the front hand well down the mast, not only

presents more sail to the fickle wind, but also increases the rig's leverage. To effect the lift, bear off onto a broader reach, and in one explosive movement, pump the sail and thrash with the trailing leg. It is imperative to keep the board balanced by keeping your body weight over the centre line, otherwise you will just return to the deep. Gain composure and replace the mast hand onto the boom. It's a good idea when trying to effect such a tricky start to watch out for any slight gusts which will help with the proceedings.

If it's possible to fly the sail, yet impossible to generate sufficient lift, there is a final resort – the ultra light wind waterstart. This method uses the principle of levers to the maximum. The sailor must hold the mast near to its base with the front hand, the back hand then grasps the foot of the sail. There are no points awarded here for a graceful mounting – scramble aboard any which way you can! It's necessary in ultra light winds continually to bear away to facilitate good lift and prevent luffing up – this method is indeed tricky.

Above: When all else fails a very light wind waterstart, hands on mast and sail can be attempted.

Below: If the wind is fickle, put the front hand well down the mast to increase the rig's pull.

Clew-first waterstart

Many a windsurfer treading water has found that a waterstart from a clew-first position can save time and face after a badly executed manoeuvre. Many shortboard transitions can leave the sailor in an ideal situation to restart clew-first. Commonly mistimed slam gybes, jump gybes, helicopter and nose tacks conclude in a similar scenario of inevitably being dumped in the water. Most often seen, however, is the over compensated carve gybe, where the sailor plops in to windward still clutching the rig. Once you have been consigned to the briny, the need to keep the rig flying should be most prominent in your mind. Get close to the board, and with one foot in position keep the nose downwind to maintain any hope of control. Present the rig to the wind in the usual manner to create the lift, the sudden increase in power may be unnerving – but hang on! Only when you are safely on the board and balancing should you contemplate flipping the rig onto its rightful tack.

The clew-first waterstart is not as simple in practice as it appears in principle. The major difficulties revolve around holding the sail fully-powered up clew-first. A useful tip is to position the cleward hand nearer to the rear boom end – all sails are extremely unstable clew-first, and almost impossible to hold close to the wind. To stand any chance of recovery the board must remain on a broad reach throughout the proceedings.

In order to get used to the clew-first feeling it is not a bad idea to try this technique on a long board in light airs. Any board, even a long course board, can be waterstarted in the clew-first position – indeed, this can be a useful time saver in a racing situation. However, it's not a wise move to attempt clew-first sailing with a large or unstable rig, with its continual draught and leech movement.

The sails which are the most comfortable in this clew-first waterstart position are wavesails. A Force 4 wind combined with a 16½ft (5m) sail make an ideal team for training.

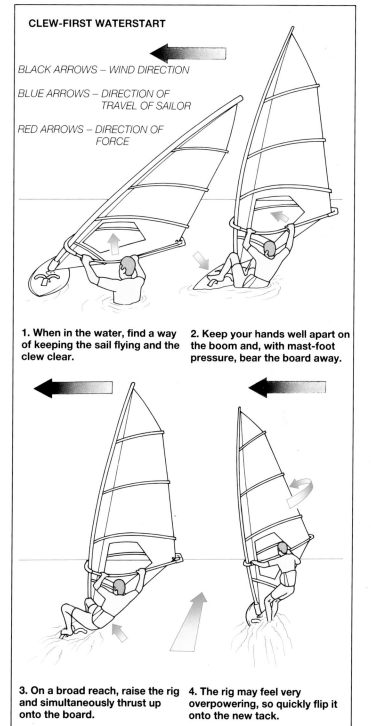

CLEW-FIRST WATERSTART

BLACK ARROWS – WIND DIRECTION

BLUE ARROWS – DIRECTION OF TRAVEL OF SAILOR

RED ARROWS – DIRECTION OF FORCE

1. When in the water, find a way of keeping the sail flying and the clew clear.

2. Keep your hands well apart on the boom and, with mast-foot pressure, bear the board away.

3. On a broad reach, raise the rig and simultaneously thrust up onto the board.

4. The rig may feel very overpowering, so quickly flip it onto the new tack.

SNAP UPHAULING

In certain situations it is useful to know how to uphaul a small board, particularly after a failed transition where the board and rig are lying in the normal uphauling position. In gentle airs this snap uphauling technique can be applied to even the smallest boards, and it can be a useful option, especially if the sailor is getting exhausted from repeated waterstart failures. It is a common sight to see World Cup sailors with uphauls attached to their boom – even in wavesailing a snappy rig pull could save the day.

Before attempting to uphaul, be sure the wind is blowing against your back and the rig is downwind; it can be an exceptionally tricky act to reposition either board or rig through 180° on a small board. With one foot in front of the straps and the other just in front of the mast, take the uphaul to aid your own balance and begin to hoist the sail. In order to maintain balance keep both feet over the board's imaginary centre line and bend your knees to lower your centre of gravity; the last point of stability is holding the top of the uphaul with the clew just in the water. In a continual movement snatch the rig cleanly out of the water and immediately sheet in to maintain balance.

As soon as the sail (which acts as an excellent counterweight) is raised, the board's balance can be precarious. Keep this in the back of your mind; don't make any sharp jerking motions which could interrupt the equilibrium and stay over the more buoyant centre part of the board to reduce sinking. A sailor can often arrive at a stance where the water is well above both knees, common on low volume boards or with heavy sailors. Provided balance is maintained this ungainly half sunken posture can be transformed into lift and planing as the power comes back on. As soon as the rig is completely clear, get the mast immediately forward while sheeting in quickly, to either refloat the board or pump up onto the plane. Simultaneously move both feet behind the mast and bear away to prevent another nose dive.

Above: With a foot either side of the mast, take the uphaul since this will act as a stabilizer.

Above right: Pull up the sail, hand over hand. Be aware that a small board may submerge.

Below left: From the top of the uphaul, pull the rig across as if to look through the front window.

Below: Grasp the boom with both hands and bear away to urge the board to the surface. These steps must be carried out rapidly as smaller boards are less stable when not moving.

THE CARVE GYBE

The carve gybe is, without exception, the single most important technique encountered in high-performance board sailing. Once mastered, the sailor will discover that many variations and refinements are possible, but at the end of the day, there are few sights more impressive than a perfectly executed standard carve gybe.

The style of the carve gybe depends largely on the prevailing conditions and on the character of the board being used. A long board gybe, for instance, is worlds apart from a technically similar transition on a waveboard. For instructional purposes we should concentrate on the most popular "recreational" classic carve gybe. This may serve as the basis on which to elaborate later in the learning processes.

Ideally, for the teething period, a board between 8½ and 9½ft (2.6 and 2.85m) capable of a strong turning circle should be used. Camber-induced rigs, at least in the early stages, should be avoided as they make the rig flip rather too violent. Similarly, large sails, above 65sq ft (6sq m) are difficult to manoeuvre. A wave-style sail of about 54sq ft (5sq m) in a Force 5 with relatively flat water is the ideal learning combination.

The carve gybe is a fully planing 180° turn, with no diminution of speed; the true test of a good gybe is the maintenance of the same speed at entry and exit. To stand any chance of success, the gybe must be attempted while fully planing, on the fastest point of sailing – a broad reach. Not without reason is the "go for it" formula so often repeated at this juncture!

To effect the carve gybe, unhook from the harness while in the reaching position. Glance ahead for a flat water area in which to make the turn, well away from other water users. Withdraw the rear foot from its strap and place it on the leeward rail. To initiate the turn, bend the knees and lean inwards and forwards. As the board carves its own arc, maintain your body position and keep the rig upright at arm's length. While heading almost

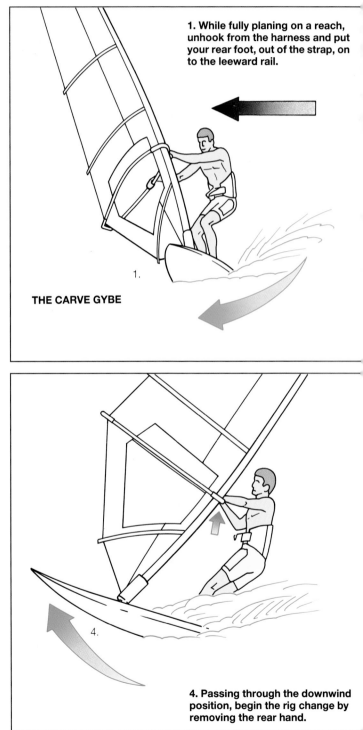

1. While fully planing on a reach, unhook from the harness and put your rear foot, out of the strap, on to the leeward rail.

THE CARVE GYBE

1.

4.

4. Passing through the downwind position, begin the rig change by removing the rear hand.

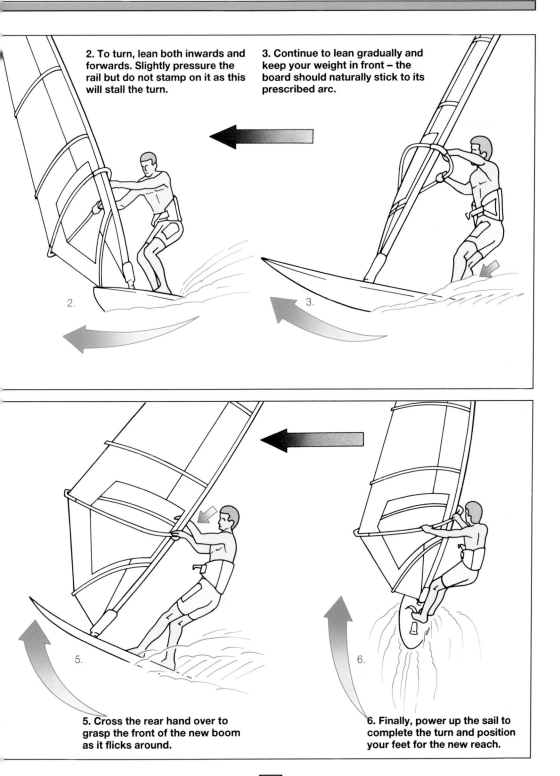

2. To turn, lean both inwards and forwards. Slightly pressure the rail but do not stamp on it as this will stall the turn.

3. Continue to lean gradually and keep your weight in front – the board should naturally stick to its prescribed arc.

2.

3.

5. Cross the rear hand over to grasp the front of the new boom as it flicks around.

6. Finally, power up the sail to complete the turn and position your feet for the new reach.

5.

6.

downwind, at speed, the rig should feel weightless. Carry out the rig change by releasing your back hand. Your front hand will act as a pivot around which the sail will automatically flip; your back hand, crossing over to take the rig on the new tack, now becomes your front hand. Now repower the sail with the back hand – only at this final stage do you change your feet over.

So much for the theory. Putting it into practice is, of course, a more difficult matter. The error most often committed is changing the feet mid gybe. This disengages the gripping rail, and the board then shoots out of its arc, taking the helpless rider on a one way trip downwind. Another mistake is entering the gybe with too little speed. You should have sufficient speed at entry to be able to complete the turn without the powered up sail –

Below: Even experts can mistime a basic gybe – practice can only make perfect!

or to put it another way – you should be able to turn the arc by board speed alone. You may also find yourself stalling the board mid gybe. People often attempt turns that are too tight for their ability, and as a result the board comes off the plane, or the sailor comes off the board. It is much easier to maintain speed around a wide arc rather than a narrow one. The board will also stall if the sailor takes the rig out of its three-dimensional plane.

Last but not least are the problems associated with the crucial rig change. It is a good idea to practise the boom-to-boom hand movements on dry land – timing the rig change is critical. In very strong airs at maximum speed you can release before the run position, although normally such an early release means the board will stop. Too late a release and the board will continue to carve up and head to wind on the new tack; even the best sailor can make a costly mistake during the basic carve gybe.

One-handed carve gybe

Like many windsurfing man-oeuvres, the one-handed gybe is more ornamental than of any great practical use. But that, in a sport where so much depends on good style, is no reason for not mastering it! It also has the effect of freeing the other hand for use as a brake. In very strong airs all boards are susceptible to breaking out from their normal turning track; trailing the inside hand commits the sailor's whole weight to the turn and provided the water is smooth, the board will stay on the rails.

In strong winds the rig must be released a little earlier. Tapping the hand on the water is effected as the board passes the dead-run position – the touching moment only has to be very short and sweet to achieve the desired effect. As the board approaches its new reach, the sailor must return to meet the boom on the new tack. A consequence of the hand-dip is that the turning arc will be tighter, so that less ground will be lost downwind.

It is possible for "funsters" with agility and dynamic balance to spin the rig while the hand is still cooling off. This alternative, radical style of gybing requires flipping the rig and catching it with the same hand. It goes without saying that very high board speed and precise co-ordination are essential.

Above: In very strong wind and flat water, the rig can be spun with the hand still brushing the water's surface.

Right: A stylish one-handed gybe can be used to good effect in strong airs as it commits the sailor and board to its arc.

CARTING THE KIT

Carrying your gear to the water's edge in strong winds is a process that requires a little forethought. Whichever method you choose, you must avoid dragging your gear along the beach. Bumping or dragging over abrasive sand, shingle and boulders will quickly reduce the life expectancy of your sailing equipment.

For convenience's sake, and to save a journey, insert the mast foot into the board. Don't pick up the whole lot any old how, or you are likely to be helicoptered around by the wind and unceremoniously dumped in a heap. First things first! Point the board and rig in the direction of travel, and always stay to windward of the sail. The most

Above right: Carrying the board and sail at your hip is the most simplistic way to travel.

Right: Holding the board at your hip with the sail on your head gives you a little more freedom.

straightforward method is to carry the board at hip-level; place the mast along the leeward rail and lift the whole lot using the front of the boom and front footstrap. You may stand either to windward or leeward of the board. In surf, standing to leeward can prevent the board from straying downwind. For a slalom beach start the hip method is by far the most popular. In situations where the surf is rolling in or there is a small beach break it may be necessary to raise the board a little higher.

To carry the sail, place one hand on the mast just below the boom, raise the rig and be prepared for it to flap. Bend down and with your spare hand use your footstrap to raise the board, resting the sail on your head. Be careful with this method – excessive head pressure on the sail, and more specifically the window, can distort the cloth.

It may be that a long trek to or from the water is inevitable. For such long distances it is easier to carry your gear above your head, leaving both legs free from any obstruction. To raise the gear, place the board upside down with the tail across the boom. While holding the front windward strap and mast, upend the equipment onto the nose and work under to effect the lift.

Once balanced, the board should sit with little strain on the sailor's head. *Do not,* repeat *not,* use this method if your board is a courseboard, or if it's heavy; you could do yourself a very nasty injury to neck or spine.

Right: Many situations arise when a long walk to and from the water is unavoidable. Lifting the whole package above the head is by far the best solution. It is advisable, however, to avoid this method if the board is heavy – irrespective of its size – or if the wind is very strong.

LAUNCHING TIME

Launching your board, especially in surf, is often one of the most challenging aspects of windsurfing, and getting it just right is often one of the most frustrating. Even the smallest of waves or beach-breaks can flip your board or body over and, depending on the conditions, can break masts, booms or more often than not, fins. With the correct approach most of these misfortunes can be avoided.

Carry your equipment into the water until there's sufficient depth for the fin, at least knee-level. Look out for steep shelving beaches which in a couple of steps could leave the water lapping around your neck! Drop the board in sufficient depth to clear the fin with your weight upon it. Hold the rig upright. Stay adjacent to the board and prevent it from luffing up by maintaining forward pressure through the mast foot — have both hands in the

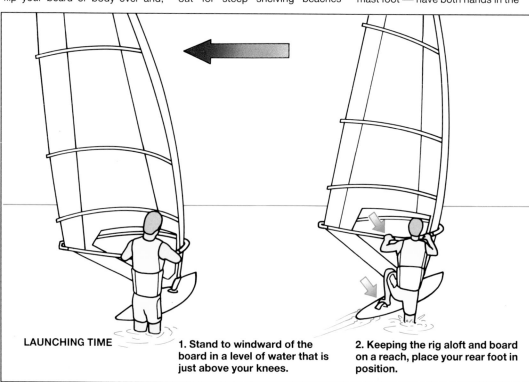

LAUNCHING TIME

1. Stand to windward of the board in a level of water that is just above your knees.

2. Keeping the rig aloft and board on a reach, place your rear foot in position.

sailing position on the boom. Place your rear foot on the board over the centre line. The stronger the wind, the further back the foot can go. Raise the rig a little in preparation for lift and simultaneously sheet in and launch yourself onto the board. Briefly ease the rig forward to bear away and gain forward motion. All that remains is to secure the sailing position and get the board planing as soon as possible.

Different conditions call for different launching techniques. Some are obviously more difficult than others. In onshore winds, for example, launching is invariably more tricky as you have to set aboard closer to the wind. In wave locations always watch the surf and try to anticipate a break in the waves. Approach oncoming waves with determination, keeping the board's nose well up. By keeping your weight back the board will ride over the white water instead of punching through it.

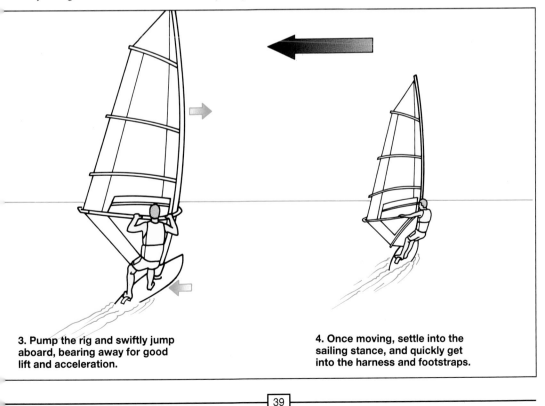

3. Pump the rig and swiftly jump aboard, bearing away for good lift and acceleration.

4. Once moving, settle into the sailing stance, and quickly get into the harness and footstraps.

CHAPTER 4

PLAYING IT SAFE

Windsurfing is a safe sport provided we use common sense and understand our sailing environment. Unfortunately there will always be incidents in which unwary sailors are caught out simply because of lack of knowledge of the sailing area or through stupidity. To "play it safe" all we need is a basic understanding of the elements and some common sense.

One of the most important of the elements is the wind. Wind is the movement of air from high pressure areas to low pressure areas. As the air rushes between highs and lows it is deflected by the rotation of the earth. As a result, in the northern hemisphere the air spirals clockwise away from the centre of a high, and anticlockwise towards the lows.

Not surprisingly the weather patterns associated with anticyclones (highs) and cyclones (lows) are different. An anticyclone brings very calm, settled weather, since the air pressure is roughly the same over a large area. A cyclone on the other hand, with a steep pressure gradient, produces very wet and windy weather. The deeper the depression, the stronger the winds.

Just as land maps mark points of equal height with contours, weather maps join points of equal pressure with isobars. The closer together they are, the steeper the pressure gradient and the greater the likelihood of wind. Closely associated with depressions are fronts (boundaries between warm and cold air sectors) which bring with them distinct weather changes. A warm front brings low cloud and persistent rain, and precedes a warm sector of air. Once the cold front follows behind it, the cloud becomes broken and higher with showers instead of persistent rain.

In the diagram the high is tracking eastwards allowing the low to move over the west coast. As the low approaches, the winds which follow the direction of the isobars, will swing southerly and increase. As the low continues north-east,

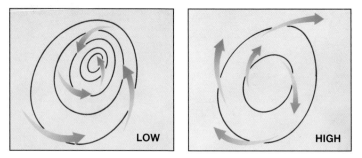

WINDS AROUND PRESSURE SYSTEMS

Winds travel anticlockwise and in towards the low pressure (cyclone) but clockwise around a high pressure (anticyclone).

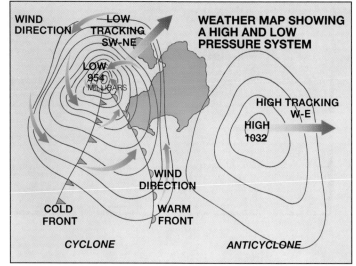

the winds will veer south-westerly but remain strong. With the passing of the cold front, the skies will clear and showers will appear. Finally as the low passes away, the winds will go westerly then north-westerly and slowly decrease.

Although large weather systems are important, there is also such a thing as local weather. For example, in hot clear weather a local sea breeze can spring up transforming a marginal breeze into a "good blow". As the land heats up faster than the sea the rising hot air produces a low pressure over the land.

Air off the sea rushes in to equalize the pressure, thus creating a sea breeze. During the night the process is reversed as the land cools faster than the sea creating a land breeze blowing out to sea.

The important factors to bear in mind when considering the wind are its strength and direction. The direction is always expressed in terms of where it comes from, thus a southerly wind comes from the south and blows in a northerly direction. Wind strength is universally measured using the Beaufort Scale, named after its inventor,

Admiral Beaufort. The scale grades the strength of wind according to the wind speed in knots. It also gives indications of what the sea state is.

Wind direction is often tricky to work out. Flags, trees or smoke give the observer onshore a rough idea but once out to sea one has to rely on one's feel for the wind. Contrary to popular belief, the wind and the clouds don't always travel in the same direction – what the wind is doing at cloud level and sea-level may be quite different.

It is worth highlighting the dangers associated with weather. The first is wind strength – always ask yourself if you are capable of handling it. Another potential problem is wind direction relative to the beach. Cross-shore winds are best for the sailor. Dangers arise while sailing in offshore conditions, since if anything goes wrong one gets blown further from safety. Offshore winds are also very deceptive. What appears to be a gentle Force 2 inshore can be a stomping Force 6 a quarter of a mile out to sea, into which one has to sail to get back to shore. However, excellent wave-sailing conditions can be found in cross-off winds. If you are going to

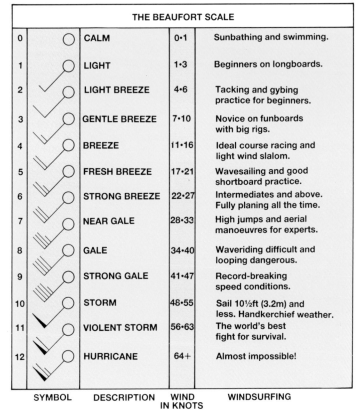

THE BEAUFORT SCALE				
0		CALM	0·1	Sunbathing and swimming.
1		LIGHT	1·3	Beginners on longboards.
2		LIGHT BREEZE	4·6	Tacking and gybing practice for beginners.
3		GENTLE BREEZE	7·10	Novice on funboards with big rigs.
4		BREEZE	11·16	Ideal course racing and light wind slalom.
5		FRESH BREEZE	17·21	Wavesailing and good shortboard practice.
6		STRONG BREEZE	22·27	Intermediates and above. Fully planing all the time.
7		NEAR GALE	28·33	High jumps and aerial manoeuvres for experts.
8		GALE	34·40	Waveriding difficult and looping dangerous.
9		STRONG GALE	41·47	Record-breaking speed conditions.
10		STORM	48·55	Sail 10½ft (3.2m) and less. Handkerchief weather.
11		VIOLENT STORM	56·63	The world's best fight for survival.
12		HURRICANE	64+	Almost impossible!
SYMBOL	DESCRIPTION	WIND IN KNOTS	WINDSURFING	

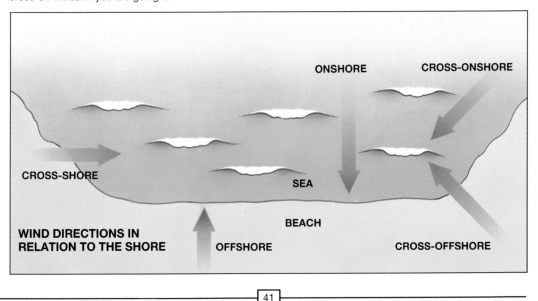

WIND DIRECTIONS IN RELATION TO THE SHORE

ONSHORE CROSS-ONSHORE CROSS-SHORE SEA BEACH OFFSHORE CROSS-OFFSHORE sail in such conditions, you must be able to sail a shortboard upwind easily and be aware of the ever present dangers.

Sailors are often hit by squalls when the wind strength and direction becomes erratic and violent. These squalls occur under a thick cloud with its own circulating air mass. Luckily there are warning signs – darker patches skimming across the water, an advancing shower and approaching thick, dark clouds. Another give-away can be the dropping of rigs and catapulting of other sailors upwind.

The dangers of fog or sea mist should be self-evident. If the visibility is poor, then don't go out, and always be aware that sea mist can descend very rapidly. Less likely, though still hazardous, are thunderstorms. Lightning striking the mast is a real possibility. If you are caught out in a thunderstorm, drop your rig in the water.

Below: Although off and heavy cross-offshore winds can be sailed, it is advisable to be careful and never sail alone.

TIDES AND CURRENTS

Anyone sailing on the sea is affected by the tide. Ignorance of the tide can be extremely dangerous. Tides are basically the vertical and horizontal movement of the water on the earth's surface, caused by the gravitational pull of the moon and sun. A tide is said to have occurred when the sea has flooded (come in) to high water and then ebbed (gone out) to low water again. During each day, two tides occur and, since the earth, moon and sun are constantly changing position in relation to one another, the tidal forces never remain constant. This results in differing high and low water marks each tide. When the earth, moon and sun are in line with one another, these tidal forces are at their greatest. The result is a spring tide which follows roughly one and a half days after the new or full moon, when the tidal range (difference between low and high water) is at its highest.

The opposite of a spring tide, a neap tide, passes roughly one and half days after the quarter moon or three-quarter moon, when the sun and moon are at right angles in relation to the earth. The smallest tidal range occurs at neap tide. The sea water flows along tidal streams while ebbing or flooding and one of the first things to realize about these currents is that they do not simply flow in and out. Nor do they flow at a constant rate, but flow at different rates depending on the state of the tide. This change in tidal flow is known as the "Rule of Twelfths" since the volume of water ebbing or flooding per hour can be measured in twelfths.

As seen in the diagram, the tide is flowing at its fastest during the third and fourth hour before or after high water. Conversely it is at its slowest an hour either side of high or low water. We also have to consider the phase of the moon. On a spring tide with the greater tidal range, there is more water movement and so a faster flow. Potentially the third and fourth hour of an ebbing spring tide are the most dangerous and should be avoided unless one is an experienced sea sailor.

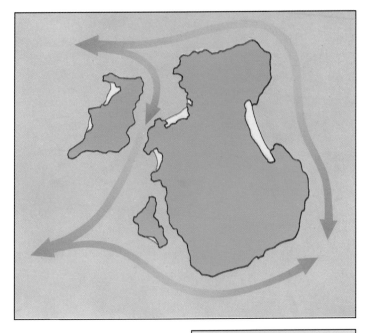

CURRENTS AT SEA

Above: Currents around land masses work in mysterious ways. The misconception is: if you are swept away on the ebbing tide, you will return to the same spot on the flooding tide.

RULE OF TWELFTHS

Below: In areas of extreme tidal flow, the safest time to sail is the hour either side of low and high water when the flow of water is at its slowest.

Rip currents are often mistaken for tidal currents, though strictly speaking they differ since they are created by breaking waves. A rip is the route the water chooses to follow once a wave has broken. However, rips can usually be identified from the beach and are therefore avoidable. If there is a section where the waves are breaking slowly or even disappearing after feathering up, the chances are that there is a rip running out at that point. Unless you feel completely confident of your sailing in the prevailing conditions, rips should be given a wide berth.

All the above factors will have a bearing on where the sailor chooses to sail. Some beaches may be unsailable on high water springs due to sea walls, others may only be sailable on springs due to underlying banks or rocks. Local knowledge is a major asset in "playing it safe", so never be afraid to ask. Take care in a wind-against-tide situation since this can change a smooth rolling swell into a confused mess.

Perhaps the most expensive tidal effect (in terms of broken gear) is caused by steeply shelving beaches. Once the tide reaches the steep incline, smooth peeling waves change into dumpers breaking in one gear-smashing close out. Timing is critical in order to get out through such a shore-break, so be warned! It is also difficult to get up a speed in these conditions. The waves are too close together and will stop the board dead.

With all these potential hazards and inherent dangers to contend with, one would be stupid to set out sailing without some idea of the state of the tide at the chosen location. Fortunately there are plenty of sources of information. Tidal predictions are given daily in the quality newspapers, and tide-tables are available from chandleries. Don't forget the Coastguard and the Harbour Master; they would much rather give you tidal advice in advance over the telephone than retrospectively from a rescue boat. With all these sources of information ready to hand, there is really no excuse for putting yourself at risk.

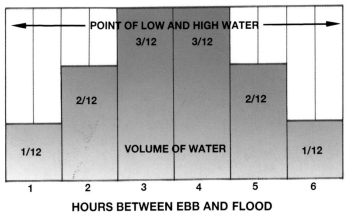

POINT OF LOW AND HIGH WATER

3/12   3/12

2/12   2/12

1/12   VOLUME OF WATER   1/12

1   2   3   4   5   6

HOURS BETWEEN EBB AND FLOOD

RIGHTS OF WAY

A performance board, in planing conditions, can be travelling at anything from 10 to 30 knots, so a crash or collision can lead to serious damage and injury. The problems multiply as popular high wind locations get crowded. It is therefore vital to realize whose responsibility it is to give way.

Some confusion over priorities arises from windsurfing itself due to the divided aspect of the sport. The racing fraternity tends to adhere to the complex IYRU (International Yacht Racing Union) rules which can take for ever and a day to read, let alone comprehend. The most basic rule, however, states, that "a vessel on a starboard tack has right of way over one on a port tack".

The port tack obviously has to give way or alter course. The rules then go on to explain priorities of windward vessels and associated racing situations.

High-performance windsurfing has its own set of rules, which in the main have little to do with racing or yacht and dinghy sailing. However, it is still important to realize that a conventional sailing vessel may ex-

Above: The sailor outward bound has the right to execute a jump without interruptions.

Below: The waveriders should steer clear and keep away from the outgoing sailor's path.

Right: The sailor nearest to the critical part of the wave has priority over other waveriders.

pect a windsurfer to give way under its rules and, clearly, it is not to a windsurfer's advantage to collide with a boat!

On inland waters, direct onshore and in dead offshore winds the starboard priority still has its applications. In general surf situations this rule has to be thrown totally out of the window. The prime surf-sailing rule is that a board going out from the beach on a jumping tack holds priority over a board coming in. The person riding in on a wave is deemed to have much more directional control and should use this ability to steer clear. It is not acceptable for a sailor to try and perform a move in front of another sailor coming out, even if he thinks it will take him well clear.

If two or more sailors find themselves on the same wave then, in general, the sailor furthest upwind has priority. As such he can begin to ride up or downwind whenever it is so desired. When it is the downwind sailor's turn to move, the options are to either get off the wave or, if the wave is long enough, ride it simultaneously away from the main sailor. A single wave can be ridden successfully by two or more sailors

provided everyone co-operates and keeps their wits about them. Making a transition onto a wave that is already occupied is not really playing the game. The sailor who picks up the wave first has priority. If someone else turns onto that wave or drops in from the back then they can expect no rights, and should keep clear even if they are to windward.

A surfing rule that has been adopted by windsurfers is that the rider nearest the peak, or critical section, of the wave has priority. This rule allows a sailor who is trying to work the best part of the wave priority over someone who appears to be wasting the opportunity and may not be attempting to ride the wave at all. Naturally there are always grey areas, but the general rule is that common sense should prevail at all times. Often, a situation may arise where a wave has more than one defined peak. The first or upwind sailor has the right to ride from peak to peak and still maintain control, even though other sailors may have initially seemed far away.

Rights of way should be considered as one set of rules to which there is no exception. In reality, however, not all water users comprehend the rules and regulations, so rely on your own common sense at all times.

To conclude, the windsurfer should always consider other water users. Unnecessary aggravation can effectively be avoided if the likes of surfers, canoeists and swimmers are kept well clear of. After all, they have their rights too! In theory any other vessel travelling under power should give way to sail. It's also worth considering that a large oil tanker is going to change course for no man!

Right: In the real world out on the water, rights of way are often confusing. Situations are not as clean cut as the theory suggests. Sometimes sailors hold a total disregard for the rules. Alternatively, fellow comrades ride a wave together, interweaving as they go.

Above: On busy days common sense is the best strategy – look about and stay aware of all the other water users!

Left: The sailor to windward (white sail) can begin to ride downwind at will, the other rider (yellow sail) must stay clear.

BASIC RULES FOR ALL WINDSURFERS

- The sailor leaving the beach has priority over the one coming in
- If two or more sailors are on the same tack, the one furthest to windward has the right of way

- The first on the wave has priority
- A sailor in the critical section should be kept clear of
- Be aware of all other water users and steer clear

COMMON SENSE AND RESCUE

Although a knowledge of the elements, and the sea in particular, make for safer sailing, the biggest factor in "playing it safe" has to be common sense. Many of the potential hazards can be avoided with a modicum of forethought – regarding weather conditions, the state of the equipment, and your own "body armour".

Make sure, first of all, that you are fit enough and capable of coping with the prevailing sea conditions. As you become more proficient, you will find that a higher

Above: Once you decide to go for a self rescue, do not ponder or hesitate as time is precious in all rescue situations. Balance yourself on the board astride the mast foot. It will be a very stable position as the rig will counteract any body movement. To begin, unplug the mast foot.

Below: The board will now be more difficult to balance upon, so steadily work along the foot of the sail towards the clew, taking out the foot batten. When recomposed, untie the outhaul rope in a similar manner to removing the boom itself.

Top right: Remove the remainder of the battens and roll the sail tightly in towards the mast. Secure the rolled rig using the uphaul and outhaul ropes.

Middle right: Position the rig roughly along the centre line of the board with the mast foot pointing in the direction of your intended goal.

Bottom right: Lie on top of the rig and begin to paddle at a steady pace. Continue towards a fixed object on the beach. Stay alert for any currents or waves that may disturb you.

level of fitness is required to sail with ease and style. Only *you* really know whether you can handle it. If in doubt, don't go out!

"Body armour", unless you are going for forward loops, simply means your wetsuit. It must keep you warm otherwise hypothermia is liable to set in, even in the summer months. Hypothermia numbs the mind and slows down the reactions, and is capable of causing severe fatigue and even death.

Just as pilots make routine checks on their aircraft, sailors should always be on the look out for wear and tear on their equipment. Fraying ropes and deteriorating universal joints must be replaced as soon as they are spotted. Check for loose rivets or cracks on the boom and ensure the board-to-rig connection is solid. Universal joint savers (reinforcements of webbing around the UJ) provide an effective short-term answer in the event of the universal joint breaking. To prevent the board and rig separating completely, always use a safety leash.

The best laid plans can of course go astray. No amount of precautions can prevent a broken boom following a catapult or broken mast in a gust. What do you do if all goes wrong? The one thing you should not do is panic! Do your best to attract attention; flares and dayglo flags will help to get you noticed. In addition you can wave your arms, shout and whistle to attract attention. If you are still unnoticed, the sail must be derigged prior to self rescue (see panel).

This method of self rescue becomes increasingly difficult as the conditions get rougher – it is not fail-safe. Should you find difficulty in making headway, rerig the sail and plug it back in to make the board more visible from the land and to reduce drift.

If you are caught in the middle of a rip or current, remember to paddle across until you are out of it. Never try to paddle against it. In surf it is possible sometimes to hitch a lift towards the beach on a wave. Be sure, however, to select small shallow waves as opposed to mast-high dumpers.

Advanced sailors should know how to rescue stranded fellow sailors. There are two methods of doing this – from alongside or from in front. To tow someone alongside, with their rig safely stowed, approach them from downwind, so that he or she can take hold of your mast foot or a footstrap with one hand while lying down. This is a very effective method in calm conditions; however, in stronger winds you will need to tow the incapacitated sailor from in front using a tow line of between 10 to 15ft (3 to 5m). The line should be tied around your mast foot, passed through the towing eye on the other board, then given to the other sailor to hang on to. It is essential that they hold the line, otherwise the sailor could get washed off the board and unwittingly left behind. Talk to the sailor if you can, and try to ensure that there is a mutual understanding.

Right: In potentially hazardous situations, a tow can come in useful. It's advisable to accept a tow especially if it's difficult to make headway. Sailing the rescue vehicle can be quite an art in itself, as you can see in this aided rescue shot.

DERIGGING PROCEDURE AT SEA

1 Sit astride the board and unplug the mast foot. Working your way along the foot and leech, take out any battens and place them up the luff tube
2 Let off the downhaul slightly then edge along the foot towards the clew. Untie the outhaul and throw the boom end towards the mast
3 Roll the sail in very tightly towards the mast. Secure the roll at the top using the outhaul and at the foot using the uphaul
4 Lie the folded rig across the board then swing it underneath of your body with the mast foot pointing to the nose of the board
5 Lie down and paddle

CHAPTER 5

TRANSITIONS AND TRICKS

Transitions and tricks can seem much the same, and it is often difficult to distinguish one from the other, since the move can be over in an instant. Theoretically, transitions are methods of proceeding from one tack to another, while a trick is a manoeuvre purely designed to catch the eye of the onlooker. Many tricks are, however, akin to some transitions, often involving similar rig changes, although throughout, the sailor stays on the same tack.

Variety is the spice of life, and nowhere more so than in this sector of the sport. There are literally hundreds of variations on the basic tricks and transitions; some actually can transform the manoeuvre completely. Thus the carve gybe, itself a basic transition, can be transposed into a one-handed, boom to boom, no-handed or even pirouette manoeuvre.

A difficulty gradient will soon be perceived by the learner; the best approach is learn to walk before you can run. The basics can be quickly grasped, but some of the variations can take years to refine. Much will depend on mental attitude. Many sailors almost talk themselves out of progression. In order to learn, time on the water must be spent constructively; the appropriate literature must be studied, and *practice* must be the watchword.

Leading exponents of transitions and tricks often combine them, or blend one into another, especially when trying to score points in competitions. This shortboard freestyle is becoming a sport in its own right, and one often sees the basic manoeuvres being supplemented or varied by a quick pirouette, sail 360° or simple hand drag. The possibilities are endless, and there is no limit to what a resourceful sailor can come up with. So go for it!

Right: Transitions and tricks can be combined, such as this basic carve gybe plus pirouette.

DUCK GYBE

In the early years, the duck gybe was regarded as the ultimate transition and, as such, was deemed exceptionally difficult. With the benefit of hindsight and better equipment, we can now see that the difficulties were exaggerated.

The odds are if you complete a duck gybe, you will exit with the board on the plane. It is this exhilarating feeling which remains the aspiration of all progressive sailors. Modern technology and innovation have made it a much easier manoeuvre to master than hitherto. One of the modern sailor's advantages is that, during any windy session, he will see the duck gybe being executed frequently and often with great panache. Seeing the man-

oeuvre performed before your eyes is one of the best ways of learning – on the simple principle of emulation: "If he can do it, then so can I!"

The duck gybe is, in principle, very similar to the carve gybe – the board control is almost identical in both cases. The most notable difference is in the rig change process. As the name suggests, the sailor ducks at the critical moment and passes the rig over the headwind turn. It used to be more difficult to sail out of a carve gybe at speed. Loss of acceleration was partly due to inferior equipment and design. Many sailors preferred to duck gybe since the sail spent less time depowered. As carve gybing and equipment improved, so exit speeds increased. Thus the carve gybe eclipsed the duck gybe. To-

day, duck gybing has no place in slalom and course racing, since the racing sail's foot roach makes ducking almost impossible. In wave and recreational sailing, however, the duck gybe is still at a premium.

As board speed is the essence of success, it is important to approach the turn fully planing. On a broad reach, look ahead for suitable flat water on which to perform the gybe; a choppy surface will make the board bounce, hampering control. Initiate the turn by depressing the inside rail with the rear foot. Be prepared for the rig change, which happens earlier around the turn than in the carve gybe. Cross over your front hand towards the rear boom end and let the back hand go. Duck under the sail as it swings over your head –

THE DUCK GYBE

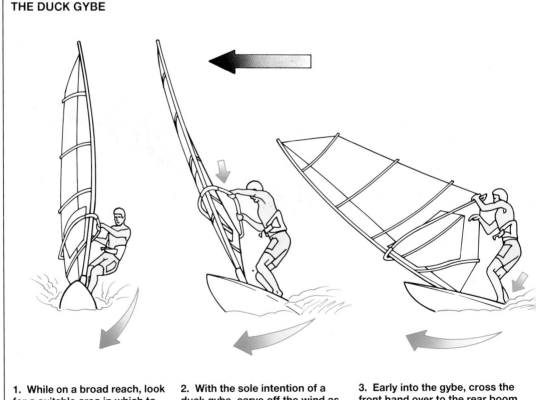

1. While on a broad reach, look for a suitable area in which to perform a duck gybe.

2. With the sole intention of a duck gybe, carve off the wind as if entering a normal carve gybe.

3. Early into the gybe, cross the front hand over to the rear boom end and release the back.

the sail will feel weightless. Maintaining the carve, throw the rig back over your shoulder to take hold of the new boom as near to the mast as possible. With both hands in the normal sailing position, sheet in and power out of the turn. Do not change your feet over until the turn is completed. At all costs, resist the temptation to slow down on entering the turn. If you do, the board will run out of steam and ignominiously stall during the duck.

The duck itself represents a major problem for many sailors. Be sure to lower your body, otherwise the mast will hit the water as you pass it over your head. Maintain your body weight inwards and slightly forwards. If you inadvertently lean back, the board will slow down. As a result, the all-important

apparent wind which makes the rig feel weightless, will shift back, whereupon the rig will then suddenly power up in mid-turn and hoist you off the deck. The action of throwing the rig over your shoulder brings the front of the new boom as near as possible.

It is imperative that the new boom is grasped near the front, or else its pull will unbalance you. With larger sails or long booms, it may be necessary to shuffle your hands along the new boom towards the front end. In stronger airs using funboard rigs, this is a habit that must be avoided if you want to achieve a perfect turn.

The faster your style of sailing is, the more chance you have of delaying the duck and therefore creating excitement for the onlookers.

One-handed duck gybe

A well executed one-handed duck gybe, tapping the water with the other hand on the turn, is indeed an impressive sight for the spectator, and very good for the morale of the performer!

Again, there are parallels to be drawn with the one-handed carve motion. In both manoeuvres, the sailor is committed to the turn, keeping the correct rail engaged throughout while simultaneously reducing the turning circle. As the sailor leans in to sweep the water, the sail will have plenty of room to pass over the sailor, avoiding the "clew sandwich" which is liable to happen in very high winds when the tail end of the rig can catch the sailor's head.

Timing is critical. With full board

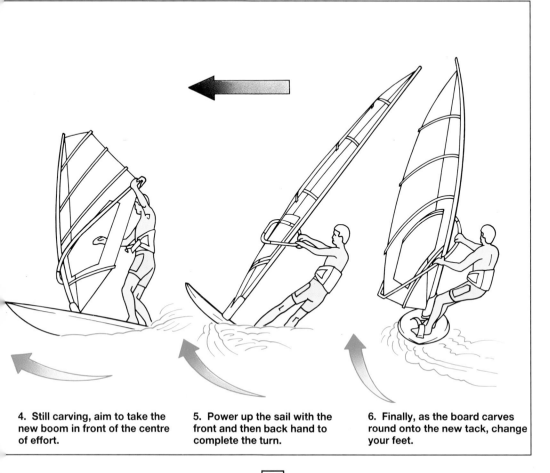

4. Still carving, aim to take the new boom in front of the centre of effort.

5. Power up the sail with the front and then back hand to complete the turn.

6. Finally, as the board carves round onto the new tack, change your feet.

speed, the sail should be ducked under as early as possible. The idea is to touch the water and to return the hand to the boom just as the board passes through the downwind position, after which the sail will automatically repower. The rig change has to be both swift and agile in order to maintain balance at high speed.

SHORTBOARD TACK

Tacking a small board is a real art. Volume and board length are critical factors which dictate the amount of skill required. It is difficult, but possible, to tack a sinker using this method; if you can pull it off you deserve congratulating.

To start, try using a 9½ft (2.85m) board, which should have sufficient volume to support your weight if the board comes to a halt. It is useful to have this margin of error offered by a floatier board. When you have mastered the technique you can try it on a smaller board.

Carve the board up into the wind, keeping your weight forward to prevent sinking the tail and stalling. Take the mast with your front hand, and position your leading foot adjacent to the mast foot. Keep your body weight over the board. Hop or shuffle quickly around the mast, positioning your old front foot down and over the centre line on the new side. Immediately sheet in and bear away – it may need a lot of front-foot and mast-foot pressure to get off the wind.

The key to success is speed and agility. The object is to tack the sail before the board has the chance to lose too much speed. The tacking process happens earlier than the normal longboard tack. Dithering at the mid-tack stage is not an option! Once you arrive on the new tack the board may, depending on its volume, be submerged. As long as the sail is sheeted in, this should create no problem.

Right: The one-handed duck gybe requires top board speed for a tidy result. An early rig change will leave more time for the split-second hand drag.

Tacking opens up many avenues of sailing. In waves, a quick tack can often get you out of the path of an oncoming wave, as well as keeping you well upwind. Occasionally in slalom, a tactical error or wind shift can often leave you downwind of a mark. Two successive tacks can quickly get the racer back on course.

SLAM GYBE

The slam or scissor gybe is one of the most practical of all transitions. It is both quick and loses little ground downwind – this is particularly important for the shortboard sailor, with his poor upwind ability.

The essence of the slam gybe is to sink the tail and pivot the board about the fin. It relates best to slalom or smaller boards.

It is easier to generate a 180° pivot from a close rather than broad reach. If fully planing, reduce your speed just prior to the turn. Begin by moving the back hand down the boom and placing your rear foot behind, and to leeward of, its respective strap. Both these actions

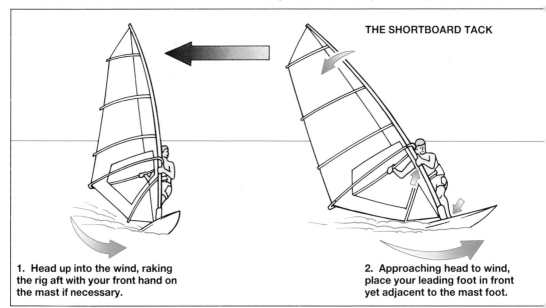

THE SHORTBOARD TACK

1. Head up into the wind, raking the rig aft with your front hand on the mast if necessary.

2. Approaching head to wind, place your leading foot in front yet adjacent to the mast foot.

Below: Initiate the slam gybe by slowing down momentarily and pointing slightly to windward.

Below right: Move your rear hand down the boom then lift the front footstrap while pushing down on

the rear leeward rail – also pull up on the boom in one quick sharp movement.

will increase your leverage. Simultaneously lift the windward rail, pressure your rear foot hard and lift up on the boom. The board will respond at once. As the board snaps around, change your foot to the new tack. Remain low to counteract the instant pull of the rig clew-first. As soon as the board has levelled out, flip the rig and power up the sail to prevent you from luffing into the wind.

The slam gybe can be performed in virtually any wind strength, and indeed, strong airs can be used as an added advantage to pivot against. As the wind increases, the time spent in the precarious clew-first position should be correspondingly reduced.

The tightness of the turn depends entirely on the nerve and commitment of the rider. The radius and speed of spin is related directly to the pressure on the board and the sharpness with which the boom is lifted. With maximum effort in these areas, the fin can be deliberately aerated, leading to the ultimate in tight, explosive gybes.

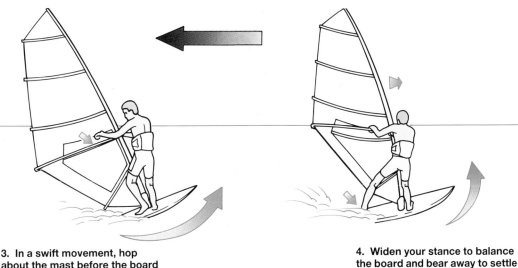

3. In a swift movement, hop about the mast before the board has had chance to stop and sink.

4. Widen your stance to balance the board and bear away to settle onto the new tack.

Below: The board will spin a 180° turn in an instance. While it is doing this, maintain a low body position to counteract the pull of the sail as you arrive in the clew-first position.

Below: Stabilize yourself clew-first for a moment, to prepare yourself to flip the rig.

HELICOPTER

Apart from the advantage of not having to shuffle around the nose of the board, the helicopter tack is not much of an advance on the conventional shortboard tack. Instead, the sailor can balance on the floatier section of the board behind the mast. The price to be paid for this privilege is that rig movement is increased and, therefore, more difficult to control – the sail has to rotate through 180°.

The helicopter tack is best practised on a slalom type machine that doesn't sink, since the board spends a large amount of time without forward motion. It is possible to pull it off on a 8½ft (2.6m) board, but don't be surprised if the board spends much of the time partially or even totally submerged.

Drive the board into the wind and rake the rig back, keeping an upright stance towards the mast foot. Pass the nose of the board through the eye of the wind. Rake the rig forward and down to push the nose away from the wind. Place both feet

Left: Initiate the helicopter tack by first raking the rig back and then driving the board hard up into the wind.

Right: Transfer the weight of your body to the front foot and then push the rig towards the nose of the board.

Middle right: Push the sail's clew through the eye of the wind while spinning the rig and swapping your feet.

Far right: Keep your weight aft and over the centre of the board. Sheet in and bear off.

NOSE TACK

The nose tack is one of the most practical of all shortboard transitions. With only a small amount of practice, a high success rate can be achieved. If a mistake is made, the day can be saved by a clew-first waterstart, highlighting, once again, how useful the basic moves can subsequently be.

The nose tack lends itself best to boards under 10ft (3.0m) in length, yet can be performed with the same ease on shorter models.

From a planing reach, head up into the wind to initiate the transition. As the board heads up, place your front foot around the mast towards the opposite rail. To maintain balance, keep the rear foot well back, over the centre line. Keeping your centre of gravity low and close to the water, depress the nose to clear the fin. At the same time, spin the nose through the wind. Move your feet around the mast until the board has spun a full 180°. To stop turning, the fin must be re-engaged. Compose yourself clew-first, then level the board out and shift behind the mast to spin the rig downwind, into the normal sailing

Far left: To perform the nose tack, head up into the wind and place your leading foot in front of and around the mast foot.

Left: Pressure the board's nose down in order to make the tail of the board spin down and away from the wind.

Right: As the fin re-engages, stabilize yourself clew-first – keep your weight low.

Far right: When you are in a comfortable position, raise yourself and spin the rig onto the new tack to sheet in.

firmly over the centre line to prevent the stationary board from toppling over. Force the sail's clew through the wind with the back hand, while simultaneously spinning your body and feet onto the new tack. Stay well up the board otherwise the tail will sink deep. Level the board out and spin the rig to arrive back into the sailing stance on the new tack.

It is a common error to put too much pressure on the rig when raking it forward; use only front-hand pressure, as any back-hand leaning will reverse the turn back to where you came from. Persist in raking the rig forward until the board is fully onto a new reach; only then can you advance on your new course. If you spin the rig too early, you'll be too close to the wind and thus have little power to sheet against.

Timing in lighter airs is not too critical, particularly on a floaty board. However, in Force 5 and beyond, co-ordination and technique have to be precise, as the helicopter is best at high speed. The pull of the rig during the spin is also extreme, so be prepared.

position. Sheet in, and you're away.

To help maintain rig control throughout, spread your hands well apart on the boom. This will be particularly useful when clew-first, since control is needed to stabilize the board.

Often a sailor approaches the tack with too upright a stance, which means that he is liable to be catapulted off as the board spins around. For better control, stay low with both knees bent until the board has gone through 180°. Only then, return to the normal sailing stance to meet the rig as it flips.

With a reasonable amount of practice, the nose tack is within any shortboarder's grasp. It can be applied in really strong winds, Force 8 and 9, with a small amount of extra difficulty. In these conditions, other shortboard tacks would be almost impossible to pull off.

For more advanced sailors, the nose tack can act as a good platform for a 360° spin. The first 180° is executed as described above, and then the board can be sailed along, tail first, temporarily. By continuing the nose rotation, it is possible to put the board back onto the initial tack.

THE 360

Not so long ago, the 360 was regarded as the most difficult of all tricks. While subsequently developed tricks may prove more difficult, it must be said that dexterity in handling board, rig and boom are nowhere displayed to better advantage than here. The carving, well-executed 360 turn still scores highly in wave contests, and offers great personal satisfaction for the rider who has mastered it.

A nice smooth area and high board speed are essential prerequisites of the 360. To execute the manoeuvre, carve the board downwind with consistent pressure on the back foot. Lay the rig to leeward with the clew towards the tail. At the half-way point, the board decelerates. To balance the board, place the front foot near the mast; the back foot should remain in position while still carving the turn. Sweep the sail aft as you approach the eye of the wind. If the board stalls, pressure the clew to force the nose of the board through the wind. Revert to an upright stance and sheet in hard. Carry on bearing away, and draw the board around until safely off the wind.

If you approach with insufficient board speed, the board may stall at the half-way point. It's almost impossible to steer the stationary board through the rest of the turn by rig pressure alone. Commonly, the sail will take the true wind and blow you over with rig on top. Concentrate hard on the carve throughout the turn. The moment you stop carving, the board will break from its arc. The critical moment is when you reposition your front foot.

Finally, don't sheet in too early, otherwise you may be head to wind, which means that your only direction of travel on a small board, will be downwind. As with all other moves, it's of paramount importance not to execute the 360 as a series of individual steps. For instructional purposes we take it step by step, but what we are looking for, in practice, is a gliding, seamless action. Think of a continual path rather than an unflowing series of steps.

Above: To carry out the 360 trick, firstly rake the rig aft and lean in as if entering a carve gybe. Continue to carve and lower the clew towards the water. Once you are three-quarters of the way around, move up towards the mast while still leaning on the rig. Stand up, sheet in and bear away for a complete 360° turn.

DUCK TACK

The duck tack, or carved duck tack to be precise, is one of the more recent shortboard transitions. Yet another product of Maui sailing, the duck tack involves carving the board into the wind via a duck of the rig, unlike the downwind gybe. The tack has very little in common with the duck gybe. The essential funboard principles of subtle rig control, foot steering, balance and timing all come together here – success in all departments is the order of the day.

To achieve a duck tack, the equipment, as ever, plays an important role. In the learning stage, a slalom type board is advisable; manoeuvrability, flotation and the ability to continue planing while the tricky rig operation takes place, are invaluable. A sail with a high clew and small foot roach will also make life easier.

The basics of the move are best practised on the face of a rolling swell or small wavelet. On a swell, the apparent wind shifts making the sail weightless. Simultaneously, the wave will keep the board in motion giving the sailor more time to manoeuvre the rig.

While planing towards the shore, initiate the turn by releasing the rear foot and carving the board into the wind. Twist your body to face the wind and switch your feet onto the opposite tack, placing one near the mast foot and the other well apart. To throw the rig, put your front hand to the rear of the boom and thrust the sail towards the water. Simultaneously, duck under the rig. As you duck under, pull the clew downwind; this enables you to catch the rig in front of its balance point. Continue to rake the rig aft to push the board through the wind. Approach the new tack, raise your body position and sheet in. Continue to bear away until you are on the new reach.

On starting this advanced tack, the sailor may feel himself to be in an alien body stance. It soon becomes apparent that this is, in fact, the least of your worries since the rig change needs to be so precise. The only way to achieve any chance of success is to concentrate on the stages until they become second nature. Remember to *carve* the board, even while passing under the rig. Stay low, with feet well apart to stabilize your balance. Once you have the new boom in your grasp, it is akin to the latter end of a 360 turn. This is a move well worth practising if you wish to achieve success.

Mastery of the duck tack opens up other possibilities. With complete confidence of rig control, the duck can be followed by sailing "front to sail", while the sailor faces the sail on the leeward side. Alternatively, you could carve the board back downwind, prior to a backside gybe, or push the sail through 360° to continue on the same tack. This will score both points and applause in any contest.

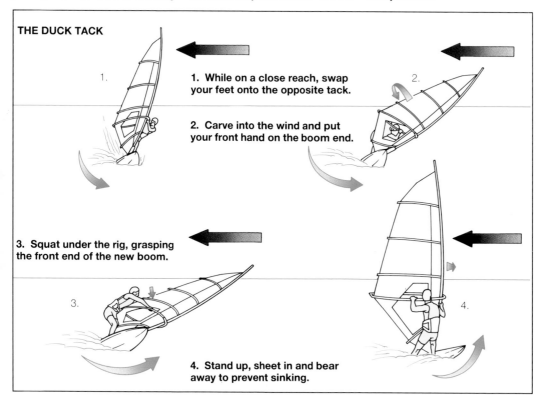

THE DUCK TACK

1. **While on a close reach, swap your feet onto the opposite tack.**

2. **Carve into the wind and put your front hand on the boom end.**

3. **Squat under the rig, grasping the front end of the new boom.**

4. **Stand up, sheet in and bear away to prevent sinking.**

CHAPTER 6

WAVESAILING

Wavesailing is the highest profile aspect of windsurfing; spectacular action and wipe-outs being exciting for spectators and participants alike. It involves three elements, namely riding, jumping and transitions. The last of these, which is incidentally the least salient factor of windsurfing, is discussed in Chapter 5. Wavejumping needs little explanation – it is certainly an aspect of the sport that most sailors aspire to. As for waveriding, this conjures up pictures of huge waves chasing over the masts of professional sailors,

usually on some amazing tropical paradise. But any wave, anywhere, can be ridden effectively, given a small amount of knowledge and the right technique.

Before setting out, it is important to assess the viability of the venue and most importantly, the wave itself. Windsurfers are luckier than surfers since they don't need to have perfectly-formed waves – good surfing waves, with strong shoulders, peeling off down a green water wall, are not often encountered. Often, waves break erratically, though for the windsurfer this

is not too much of a problem, as he can always head elsewhere in search of better conditions.

Waves are often unpredictable, being formed by wind or by the ocean's swell. It is not so good if there is a lot of white water, or if they run at an angle close to that of the wind. For good conditions to prevail, there must be a ground swell formed by a weather depression offshore. As the swell hits the beach or shallow water, its energy is released into a steep-faced wave, whose angle may be totally unrelated to the wind direction.

There are three possible wind versus wave scenarios, within which the waverider can quite reasonably operate – cross-onshore, cross-shore and cross-offshore. The wavesailor's ideal is to find side or cross-shore wind, where both jumping and riding can be performed in perfect harmony. All variations on jumps can be executed with a stiff side-shore wind. In terms of riding, the sailor can just as easily ride the waves upwind (backside) or downwind (frontside).

The more onshore the wind swings relative to the waves, the more difficult it becomes to perform a full selection of jumps. In these conditions, chop hops (see section on Jumping) and long flat jumps are the easiest to perform. A downwind ride can leave the sailor stalling at the top turn, while riding upwind is exceptionally natural and easy. A cross-off wind combined with large waves can create difficult conditions; crossing the white water is difficult, and a gust tends to hit you immediately after take-off on jumps. Waveriding, however, is a possibility; a speedy downwind bottom turn can be delivered on a wave often smoothed out by the wind. Top turns, with so much board speed, can be snappily executed, and often result in an "aerial off-the-lip" (explained later). An upwind ride is almost impossible; when dropping down the waveface, you're nearly into the wind.

Below: Waveriding is the purest element of windsurfing. The path taken along the wave is purely down to the individual and how each wave is perceived. It is more of an artform than a sport.

WAVERIDING

Gybing onto the wave

Catching a wave entails both fore-thought and skill. Firstly, the size and shape of the wave must be considered. It is very difficult to make a transition onto a breaking, or critical, section of a wave. It is more sensible to sail out of the break and perform a transition on a swell. Gybing onto a swell requires less skill in terms of the transition; if you make a mistake, you have the chance to recover. This is a much more attractive option than having to waterstart with a wave crashing down on your head.

Obviously the transition you choose will depend on your confidence and your board speed. A slam gybe is not a bad choice in lighter airs. If really planing, a carve gybe may be a better option. The secret is to pick your intended wave and to gybe early. You must try and initiate the turn in the "trough" (the channel between waves), prior to the oncoming wave or swell. When gybing at the base of the wave, an early backhand release will aid control on exit, whereupon the wave will naturally accelerate your board as it picks you up under its momentum.

Timing is critical. A late gybe will result in the sailor overshooting the face of the wave in mid-turn, there-by not only missing the wave, but often wiping out in the process. With practice it becomes possible to gybe later, and on steeper sections of the wave. The possibilities are endless; almost any transition or trick can be adapted to pick up a wave. Often, a transition mastered on flat water will require much more study and practice before it can be successfully performed on a wave.

Bottom turn

Once the wave has been caught, it is time to start riding it. The object of the exercise is to move up and down the wave's face, and in and out of the wave's more critical sections. A sailor, who drops down the face and continues on in a straight line, is not deemed to be a wave-

rider, and is often regarded as a nuisance, getting in the way of other performers.

The bottom turn is the first manoeuvre after dropping on to the face, involving a turn at the wave's base to redirect the board back up the wave ready for the top turn. The speed and projection of the bottom turn will dictate the quality of the top turn, so it's very important to point the board accurately either to continue the ride or escape from the wave.

As you shoot down the face, the board's speed will increase dramatically. You must decide quickly which direction you want to take. The backside option is the easier, as it occurs at slower speed. As you reach the base of the wave, shift your weight back. By doing this, together with raking the rig aft, the board will stall. Redirect the board up the face with hard pressure on the windward rail. The greater the application of pressure, the harder the turn.

The frontside bottom turn is initiated in a similar manner to a gybe – carving the board away from the wind. If you prefer, you may use a rear footstrap positioned for riding, so that both feet are firmly attached to the board. Otherwise, drive the board into the turn with a free foot on the leeward rail. To maintain as much board speed as possible, sheet in, tilt the rig aft a touch, and keep your weight forward through mast-foot pressure. The harder you lean and sheet in, the tighter the frontside turn.

At all times stay aware of the wave. It's suicidal to project the board into a part of the wave that has just broken. Chop or ripples on the wave can also seriously affect your turn. Hitting such chop at speed, and in a turning motion, can result in spin-out or the board bouncing. If the wave is big, this could be nasty for you. Look at the turning surface and assess how tight a turn is possible. You must think defensively!

Left: Gybing onto a wave can be made easier if the turn is initiated as early as possible.

Top: Cutting a backside bottom turn involves heading upwind along the face.

Above: A frontside bottom turn directs the board away from the wind, more than a backside turn.

Top turns; off-the-lip

The top turn, or off-the-lip, is the most exciting aspect of waveriding from both the rider's, and the spectator's point of view. After the bottom turn has directed the board up the waveface, the object of the top turn is to change direction, once again, back down the face in order to continue or complete a ride.

As with the bottom turn, the top turn has its corresponding front and backsides. To redirect the board from a backside bottom turn: bear down on the opposite leeward rail, bear away and lean in towards the rig. The board should then regain speed and drop down the face.

The frontside top turn or "re-entry" is a much more snappy affair. The board's speed, following the bottom turn, is used to create a tight turning motion at the top of the wave. Timing is critical – bad timing often results in a drop over the back of the wave. To simplify matters – try an early turn. Lean back and pressure the inside rail.

As you begin to turn, tilt the rig back and remain sheeted in. As the board faces back down the wave, relieve the foot pressure to prevent spin-out.

A gentle top turn is the best starting point, though the goal is to eventually leave the top turn at the last moment, and force the board back around using the added power of the wave's lip. To achieve the full 180° redirection, the off-the-lip requires split-second timing and total commitment. A variation of this is the one-handed top turn which shortens the arc of the turn to create an impressive sight.

Riding the wave is often regarded as an artform – and so indeed it is, when perfectly carried out. To achieve perfect timing and to gain a knowledge of the waves can take much practice; the best way is to persevere in small waves until you are both confident and competent to attempt it in bigger waves.

Left: Bear away from the top of the wave in order to execute a backside top turn.

Below: A frontside top turn redirects the board back towards the wind and down the waveface.

Above: A top turn executed at the most critical point of the wave is called an off-the-lip. Timing is particularly crucial – too late and you may easily slip over the back of the wave.

Below: A one-handed top turn or off-the-lip involves a split-second tap of the water.

Aerial off-the-lip

The aerial off-the-lip is the ultimate of all top turns in terms of difficulty. The fundamental prerequisite of an aerial is good board speed. Therefore, the bottom turn must be executed both swiftly and tightly.

A backside aerial relates more to a chop hop – redirecting the board off the wind and down the face. Landing is relatively easy in comparison to its frontside version. This can be performed in a cross-shore wind, however, it is easier in a cross-onshore when the board maintains more backside speed.

To aerial frontside, you must turn sharply enough at the wave's base, to project as vertically as possible up the face. Look for a steep critical section of wave to aerial off. Just prior to hitting the lip, depress the inner rail as hard as possible; a riding strap for your rear foot will help proceedings. Keep sheeted in and lift with your front foot. As the board spins its 180°, it will leave the wave and automatically reproject itself down the face. To land, relieve the turning pressure of your rear foot and, if necessary, sheet out a little as you land to take pressure off the fin.

The height of an aerial will depend mostly on the board's entry speed, the timing and the tuning technique at the top. The most vulnerable position is in the air; it is at this point that most radical aerial attempts are aborted. Exaggerating the turning movement in the air is a common mistake. Although it looks radical, often the board over rotates into wind, or spins out on landing. Either of these eventualities results in a cycle of rinse and spin in the wave machine.

To make it easier when performing the aerial, you need to have ideal conditions. A frontside aerial best suits a cross-offshore wind and, as mentioned, a backside aerial best suits a cross-onshore. Either way, project the board off a section of white water to aid lift.

Right: With reasonable board speed, it's not difficult to almost chop hop the board out of the top turn to get an aerial.

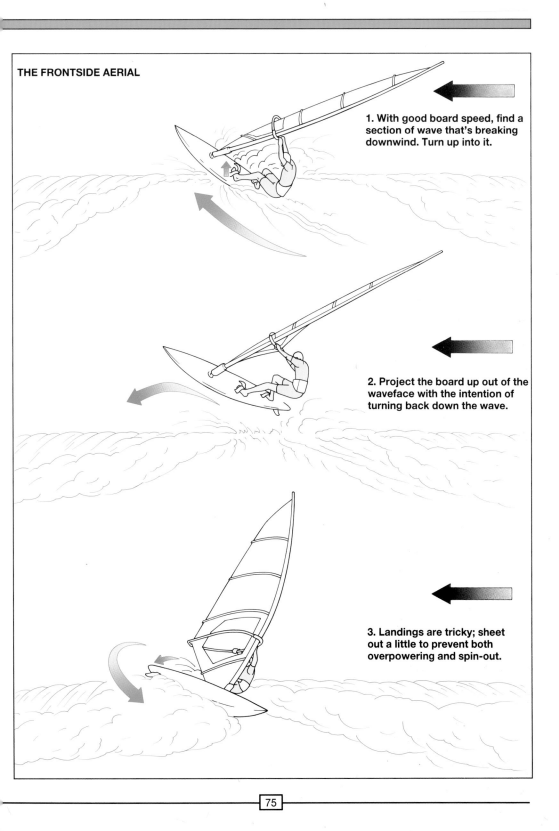

THE FRONTSIDE AERIAL

1. With good board speed, find a section of wave that's breaking downwind. Turn up into it.

2. Project the board up out of the waveface with the intention of turning back down the wave.

3. Landings are tricky; sheet out a little to prevent both overpowering and spin-out.

JUMPING

Chop hop

The chop hop is the most basic of all jumps, and acts as a stepping stone for other aerial antics later in life. In the ideal world, a steady wind and oncoming wave form the ideal learning combination. However, a good jumping technique can be acquired on flat and even inland waters, provided body, rig and board are well co-ordinated.

Some advance planning is needed to get airborne. Obviously, the faster you're travelling, the more forward momentum you have to aid lift. Watch the water ahead for signs of the slightest ramp to gain lift – even if it is only a minute piece of chop. Unhook from the harness and psyche yourself up for an explosive leap.

As the front of the board hits the chop, raise up with both front hand and leg to initiate lift. Sheet in and raise your rear foot as the tail leaves the chop. Present the board to the wind to gain wind-assisted lift. Level out by bearing away a touch and lifting the rear leg further up and into the wind. In order to land nose first, apply minimal mast-foot pressure. Straighten out your rear leg on touchdown to prevent making a catapult.

At the first attempt, jumping will appear to be disconcertingly uncontrolled. Getting airborne is the easy bit; the complications arise in flight control and landing. While in the air, control is almost exclusively governed by rig action. Remain sheeted in at all times; if you sheet out you will shorten the flight, and end up landing tail first, or (which is worse) flat. If you neglect to bring the tail to windward, so that the nose touches down a fraction downwind of the tail, spin-out is liable to occur. Keep thinking throughout the jump. With practical skill at chop hopping, a long flat jump should be within most sailors' grasp. The chop hop can be applied to longer and higher jumps of a similar trajectory at a later stage.

The risk of damage to equipment and sailor increases proportionately to flight time. A bad landing

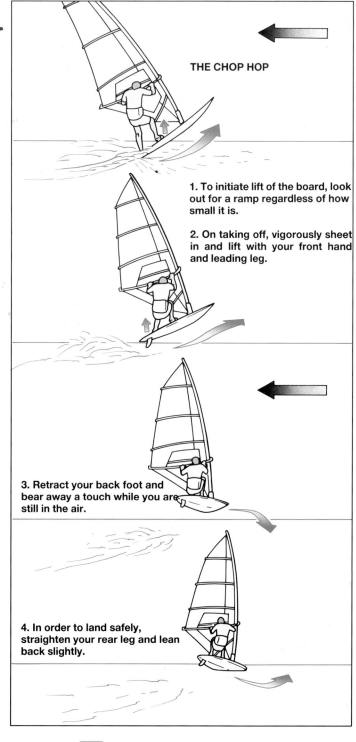

THE CHOP HOP

1. To initiate lift of the board, look out for a ramp regardless of how small it is.

2. On taking off, vigorously sheet in and lift with your front hand and leading leg.

3. Retract your back foot and bear away a touch while you are still in the air.

4. In order to land safely, straighten your rear leg and lean back slightly.

from a high, long jump can easily snap a board in two, or result in a bad catapult fall. Situations do arise when, through a lack of concentration or some external factor such as a sudden gust, control in the air is lost. If things begin to go wrong – it's time to bail out; better to live to fight another day! Always attempt to fall to windward, as you will then drop vertically, clear of rig and board which will land downwind.

Upside down

To coin a phrase, the upside-down manoeuvre can be a big turning point in a windsurfer's career. Physically, it is not difficult to pull off; the difficulty lies in effecting a good landing.

For the upside downer, a side-shore wind strong enough to allow full planing, and a steep ramp, are the best conditions. Approach the waveface at maximum speed, heading for its steepest section. As the nose of the board leaves the wave, incline your body back. When the tail follows, pull up with the front foot and push your rear foot slightly into the wind. The rig will naturally invert, and the board point skywards. Remain sheeted in to maintain control at the high point of the jump. At this stage you should be hanging under the rig, possibly with the mast tip in or above the waveface. Often, the tip of the mast may slam into the wave underneath you, so be prepared and hold on tight.

For a small upside-down jump it is easier to remain sheeted in and parachute back to the water, landing tail first. With more height, in very strong winds, it is possible to sheet in hard on descent, and execute a nose-dive entry.

A common mistake is to invert the board too late, whereupon you lose flight and height, and have no time to execute a good landing. In fact, you will probably land in the upside-down position. Overall, this style of jump is quite safe; since the board's forward motion is transferred to a vertical plane – the landing is therefore not as harsh as in some other jumps.

Below left: A long high flat jump is exactly the same procedure as a chop hop – the extra height and length is created by a wave.

Below: To get into the upside-down position, lean back just prior to take-off and hang on under the sail as it inverts.

Table top

Aerial contortions are nowhere more spectacularly exhibited than in the table top. This entails twisting the hull skywards; variations of it go by several names – donkey or mule kicks, or flare jumps.

For a table top to be successful, good height above the wave is essential, since air time is needed for the inversion. So, once again, head at speed for a critical part of the wave in order to get maximum height out of it.

Once you have decided on a table top, put as much effort as possible into the jump. Do not (as with the upside downer) lean back. As you rise, push your back foot hard into the wind and above your head. Keep the rig horizontal to the

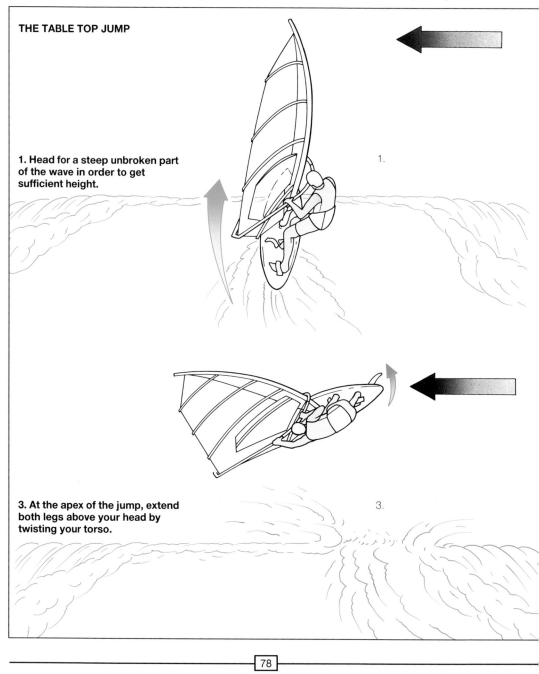

THE TABLE TOP JUMP

1. Head for a steep unbroken part of the wave in order to get sufficient height.

1.

3. At the apex of the jump, extend both legs above your head by twisting your torso.

3.

water. At the apex of the jump, extend both feet skywards. The back foot must point nearest to the wind. The board will now be inverted. Snap the board back under your body, still sheeted in, and execute your landing. By putting pressure on the mast foot via the rig, the board will level out in midair. Using your feet, angle the board slightly away from the wind for touchdown.

As you gain confidence you will find that, with greater height, a slight hover in the apex position can be managed. But don't linger too long, otherwise you will lose your chance of making a successful landing. During initial attempts, try to make the inversion as quick and snappy as possible.

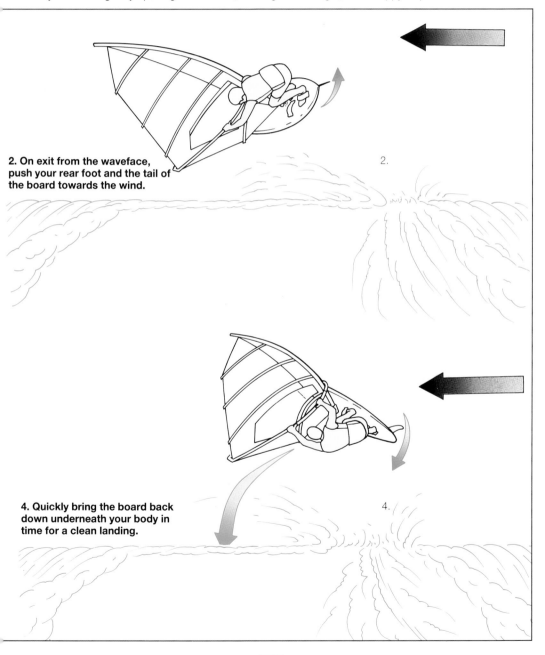

2. On exit from the waveface, push your rear foot and the tail of the board towards the wind.

2.

4. Quickly bring the board back down underneath your body in time for a clean landing.

4.

Barrel roll

The barrel roll, a variation of the backward loop, is the most traditional of all the loops. The principle involves a spiral motion up and into the wind, passing the nose of the board through the wind and down to land. The rotating motion is initiated before the board leaves its ramp. The board can take many paths through the rotation, from a horizontal to a more vertical mode, depending on the wind and the steepness of the wave. The more vertical rotations are much harder to land. You should be proficient at landing nose first and upside-down jumps before trying this.

Carve the board up into the wind as you go up the face of the wave. Lean back a little, and as you leave the wave, sheet in vigorously and throw your weight in the direction of the rotation.

The board will pass through the eye of the wind. Pull the clew of the sail through the wind and remain

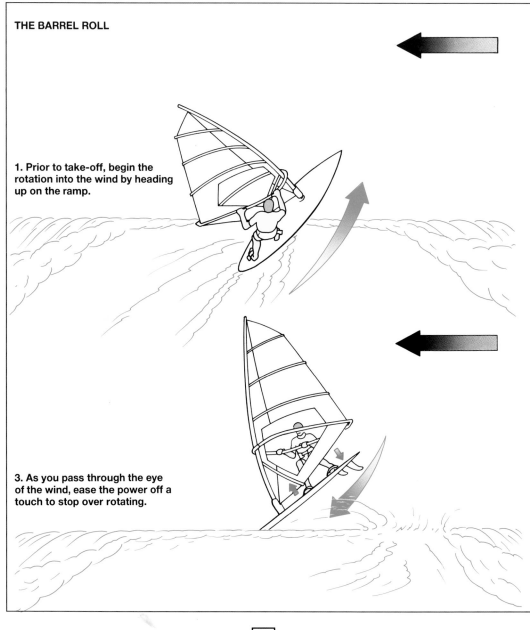

THE BARREL ROLL

1. Prior to take-off, begin the rotation into the wind by heading up on the ramp.

3. As you pass through the eye of the wind, ease the power off a touch to stop over rotating.

sheeted in to continue the rotation. Aim to land nose first on a broad reach. It may be necessary to sheet out a little to stop the rig's immense pull and to avoid over rotating.

Starting the spinning motion of this loop is relatively easy, and should be within the grasp of every reasonable jumper. Controlling the spin to land is where the problem lies, which explains why very few perfect barrel rolls are seen, and why a higher loop of slower rotation offers you much better chances of a successful landing and a well-executed barrel roll.

Often you will see a sailor head into wind and stop, plummeting down after only half a rotation. Commitment and body weight have to be used to good effect. Force your weight purposefully about an imaginary axis, to project the board about the tricky third quarter of the manoeuvre. Initially, good landings may be down to luck rather than good judgement.

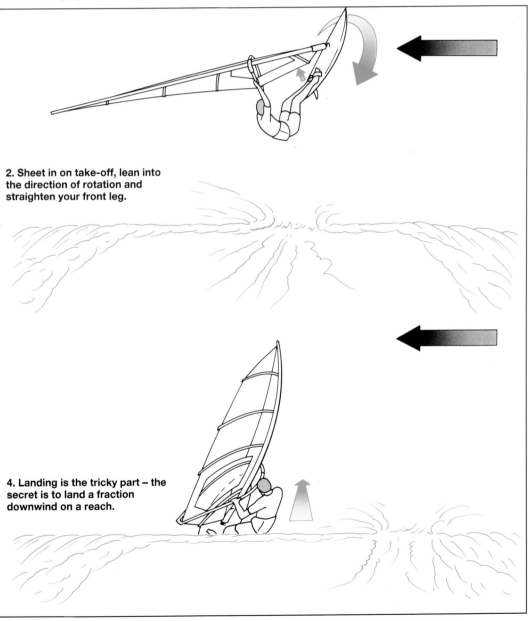

2. Sheet in on take-off, lean into the direction of rotation and straighten your front leg.

4. Landing is the tricky part – the secret is to land a fraction downwind on a reach.

Forward roll

The forward roll is another looping-type motion, but it is far removed from the barrel roll/backward loop, and should not be confused with it. It is sometimes denominated a Cesare or Cantagalli roll, after its Italian pioneer – Cesare Cantagalli.

Of all the jumps covered so far, this is potentially the most hazar-dous, since there is a point where the bail-out option doesn't exist. Complete commitment, coupled with perfect technique, are the only ways of avoiding danger.

For first attempts, bear away prior to take-off, in order to gain speed and partial rotation. As you leave the wave, sheet in and draw the rig aft, so that the tip points to the shore. Lean your leading shoulder forward and pull your rear foot over your head. You must hang on tight in this vulnerable position. Keep leaning forward as if to look around the front of the mast. The clew will come through the wind, and you will drop from above to hang below the boom. At this point of the roll, the danger is over. If you

maintain composure, you will almost parachute down and land with no difficulty at all.

There are certain conditions which lend themselves to learning. Start off with small waves, 3 to 4ft (1 to 1.2m) high, and a cross-shore wind Force 4 to 5. Too small a wave will leave you with a lack of height. Watch out for strong and gusty conditions which can often cause over rotation, and a possible collision which may well damage your equipment.

The most common mistake, however, is the "half roll"; landing in this position can be very painful and injurious – it is a wise precaution to use body protection. Next time, lean in and sheet in harder.

Left to right: Initiate a forward roll well before take-off. On the approach, bear off to pick up speed and sheet in. On take-off, direct the rig back towards the beach, keeping both knees bent. Continue to lean, as if to fall shoulder first over the mast. The clew of the sail will blow over and force you down to land.

CHAPTER 7

THE RACING GAME

Racing was introduced into windsurfing at a very early stage. Initially it involved mainly longboard racing, using regatta sails and flatboards around a traditional yachting triangle course.

Funboard sailors soon made their presence felt, and racing became possible in higher winds. Today's funboards are hybrid machines which excel in strong wind conditions; this makes racing fast and exciting for competitors and spectators alike.

"It's just a game!" declared Britain's Dave Perks after his amateur world championship success. So indeed it is; as in chess, game strategy and tactics are necessary. Obviously the thinking has to be equally matched by windsurfing skills of board speed and personal agility to achieve success.

Strategy is the game plan of

figuring out the course and the shortest route around it. Tactics are more a matter of responding to other racers, keeping your own route trouble free and overcoming obstacles which threaten your position or obstruct your path.

Any race involves the separate components of starts, straights, and turns. Without a knowledge of these aspects and the variables of wind and water, your racing career won't advance very far. Theory, essential in its own right, needs to be coupled with practical knowledge – only gained by practice.

Below: The start of a course race is a colourful spectacle. Underlying this picturesque façade is a serious game. Just prior to the off, concentration is at its peak for the racers. Achieving is what is uppermost in their minds.

COURSE RACING

The course

The funboard course is designed to favour reaching, since that is what raceboards traditionally do best, and sailors enjoy doing the most. In effect, the course offers 75 per cent reaching and 25 per cent upwind work. The course is laid out as in "The Flattened Triangle Course". An upwind leg at the start is followed by a rapid succession of reaching and gybing back to the start. In most cases two laps of the course are required, but that is at the discretion of the race committee; it could be one, three or even four legs, depending on the size of the course and prevailing conditions. All information about the number of rounds and the way to go round (whether the buoys are to be positioned to port or starboard) is contained in the sailing instructions issued before the contest. Any amendments will be found on the official notice board. The skippers' meeting prior to the start of racing each day will confirm this.

The start

The start, along with the first windward leg, is the critical component in the overall strategy. Races can be won and lost on a start line. That's not to say that a bad start means you are out of the reckoning, but those that get a good start already have two distinct advantages – clean wind and clear water. Dirty wind from other people's sails and confused water from other boards are detrimental influences; avoid them if you can.

How then to assure a good start? The first thing to consider is the amount of bias on the line i.e. which end of the start line is closer to the windward mark – your first port of call. Race committees rarely lay a square line, either the port or starboard end has a degree of bias and this needs to be calculated. There are various ways of doing this. One way is to sit on the start line with the nose of the board pointing to a buoy at one end, and the tail of the board pointing to the other end. Then just let the sail flap freely; the

clew of the sail should point to one end or the other. The end of the line with the favourable bias is the one opposite the end to which the sail clew is pointing.

If the line is square the clew will be at 90° to the board. Another way (which requires an honest partner!) is for two sailors of similar speed to start out at opposite ends of the line on opposite tacks. The one ahead at the crossover point started from the end with the bias.

The next point to consider is the exact position of the line itself which is, of course, invisible; if you get it wrong you will incur a disqualification. Line up the buoy, the mast on the committee boat, and a fixed point on land beyond the mast, in front of you. Moveable objects, such as cars, are not recommended! Once you have established a fixed point you can refer to it by just lining up the committee boat mast to it; you will find this an essential exercise just before the start.

The starting procedure can be a complicated matter. There are usually written instructions to be taken in conjunction with the visual and audio signals that mark the start. You will hear four signals and see three different flags. Initially you will receive a preparatory signal telling you that there are so many minutes to the start. A flag will be hoisted simultaneously on the committee boat; its colour may be recognized from the sailing instruc-

Above: Practice makes perfect, as this racer reaches up and down in the Maui sunshine.

tions. Three minutes later comes the warning signal. The six minute flag will be lowered and replaced by the three minute flag simultaneously with the sound signal. Two minutes later there will be a one minute signal; the three minute flag remains flying. The final signal is the start itself – all flags are now lowered, and you should be on your way. Should anyone start prematurely, they will be spotted by the committee boat and recalled. This is signalled by a single blast after the start and a verbal recall. Failure on the part of the offender to return to the line and restart will result in disqualification. In the event of a confusingly large number of sailors being premature, two sound signals will be heard after the start, whereupon the whole process will be repeated.

The upwind leg

Your primary objective now is to arrive at the windward mark in the lead, and in a position to attack the first reaching leg in clean air. To overtake on a reaching leg is more difficult than it appears. More positions are traded on the windward leg than anywhere else. If you are racing close to the shore, the wind direction will be affected by the land; the wind will always try and cross at a perpendicular. A fixed bend in the wind can, of course, be used to advantage. Likewise, if there is a promontory, such as a pier or headland, the wind will bend around it. Recognition of these factors will help your overall strategy.

Negatively speaking, obstructions on the shore and on the water cast wind shadows. To be aware of what's happening, apply the rule of thumb! Hold out your thumb at arm's length and look down it. The obstruction should be apparently smaller than your thumb. If the obstruction is apparently bigger, you will be liable to wind shadow.

Bear in mind the problems which the tide can pose, as discussed in Chapter 4. These considerations, again, will form part of your strategy. The tactical part of the windward leg comes with recognizing wind shifts and using the rulebook to your advantage. Wind shifts are

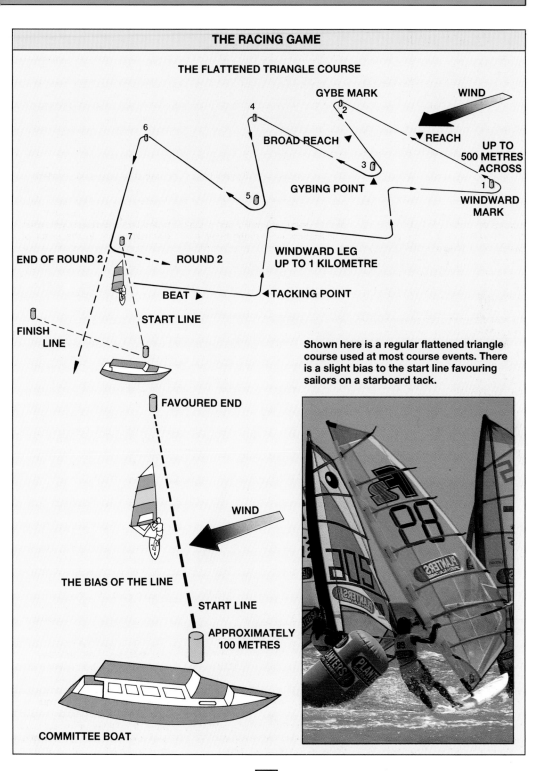

THE FLATTENED TRIANGLE COURSE

GYBE MARK

WIND

4

2

BROAD REACH ▼

▼ REACH

UP TO
500 METRES
ACROSS

3

6

GYBING POINT

5

1

WINDWARD
MARK

7

END OF ROUND 2

ROUND 2

WINDWARD LEG
UP TO 1 KILOMETRE

BEAT ▶

◀ TACKING POINT

START LINE

FINISH
LINE

Shown here is a regular flattened triangle
course used at most course events. There
is a slight bias to the start line favouring
sailors on a starboard tack.

FAVOURED END

WIND

THE BIAS OF THE LINE

START LINE

APPROXIMATELY
100 METRES

COMMITTEE BOAT

variations in wind direction which happen all the time. If you are heading upwind, and a gust hits you and you find yourself pointing lower than before, you are being adversely "headed". Conversely, if you find yourself pointing higher, you are being "lifted". Naturally, lifts are much more useful than headers and, as such, are important factors to be considered.

To suggest that you should use the rules to your own advantage may sound like gamesmanship. Though one has to say that in sailing sports this happens all the time. It is essential, therefore, that every racing sailor should know the rules and be able to apply them. What might seem a lost cause can be turned into a victory by correct and clever use of the rules.

Let us now consider the next problem – approaching the windward mark. The chances are that a lot of boards will be bunched together. It is important not to overstand the mark, that is, to sail further to windward than the mark. The approach to the mark is called making your lay line, or, the final tack up to the mark. Generally speaking, this should not be attempted on port tack, since any boards coming into the mark on starboard tack will have right of way, which could leave you waiting for a gap to break through. If you hit your lay line too early in the windward leg, any deviations in wind direction or tidal change could leave you floundering in no man's land a long way off course.

Having reached the windward mark, bear off, kick up the daggerboard, slide back the mast track, give the board and sail a few pumps, step into the back straps and head off down the first reaching leg.

Left: To drive a courseboard upwind, rail the hull to windward using the board's length to point high into the wind.

Right: To sail on a reach, aim to plane on a reduced wetted area. Get into the rear straps with the mast track aft.

The reaching leg

The main priority in the reaching leg is to blast downwind as fast as you can. There are things to look out for though, such as wind shadows from other sails, tide and dirty water conditions. To get the maximum board speed, there are some general techniques that will help. Closing the gap between the foot of the sail and the board reduces the amount of wind lost and turbulence around the foot of the sail. Applying pressure to the fin via your back foot increases speed; however, it also steps up the chance of spin-out. Moving your weight onto your back foot reduces the wetted surface area over the board – less board in the water, less drag. It also engages the leeward rail of the board for more grip. By keeping your weight on your back foot, the rig has more chance of staying upright, thus presenting more sail to the wind. Keep your body away from the rig in order to not disturb the air flow over the sail.

Some competitive sailors cultivate a fast style and stance for racing purposes. This may look ungainly and uncomfortable, but the important factor is that it works.

The raceboard stance

Rounding a buoy on a longboard may seem a fairly simple matter that calls for little discussion. However, a badly executed manoeuvre can mean lost ground and another competitor stealing your first position.

The mark should be approached at full speed with the daggerboard up and mast track back. The idea is to carve the board on the plane around the mark; this turn should not be confused with the conventional, lower wind flare gybe, which is usually learned at an earlier stage. As you approach the mark, look to see if there is anybody else in the immediate vicinity. To retain right of way you must have a com-plete overlap of at least two board lengths before the mark itself. Only then can you attempt your turn without obstruction.

With your front foot in the rear strap and back foot behind on the leeward rail, carve the board into the turn. Continue to carve with consistent back foot pressure – the back third of the board is the part which carves around. Keep your torso upright but body weight committed to the inside of the turn through the mast foot. On the new tack, immediately change your feet, stepping forwards a touch to level the board out. Spin the rig, pulling it across the body so you can sheet in quickly before the board decelerates off the plane.

Penalties

Most disputes can be resolved on the water and need never be taken further. A rule infringement on another sailor can be settled by the guilty party performing a 720° turn. The alternative to a 720°, along with any major rule infringement, is a protest whereby either the fouled person or a third party can take his case to a panel known as the protest committee. This committee will hear all sides of the story from the parties involved. They will cross-examine any witnesses, discuss it between themselves – applying the necessary rules – then take appropriate action. If someone is found guilty, it usually results in their disqualification.

Clockwise sequence: To initiate a longboard carve gybe, bear away, have the mast track back and aim initially to take a wide arc. Carve the board through the wind. Keep your body weight low and your torso upright. Swap over feet on approaching the new tack. Finally, flip the rig and, without hesitation, sheet in to power up the sail and plane out of the gybe.

SLALOM

The course

In slalom, the course is much less elaborate than in course racing. All marks are laid on fast points of sailing – either close or broad reaches. This makes for a clean cut race of only straight lines and gybing. Tacking is not necessary, as there is no upwind work.

There are two types of course, commonly known as "Ins and Outs" and the downwind "M". "Ins and Outs" is the easier course to lay, as it involves only two buoys, around which competitors have to weave a figure of eight. Races generally consist of two or three laps. The drawbacks attached to this type of course are, firstly, that spectators sometimes have difficulty seeing who is in the lead and, secondly, slight wind shifts can leave one of the marks so far to windward that it becomes quite impossible to beat towards it on a shortboard.

The downwind "M" course is increasingly popular. This consists of broad reaches off the wind, and a series of five gybes. The advantages of this course are that a slight wind shift will only change a broad reach into a close reach on one tack and make a broader reach on the other; in either case racing is unaffected. A race director will often start another round while competitors from a previous heat are further down the course.

Ideally the reaches should be between 330 and 440yds (300 and 400m) in length. Heats are run on a single or double elimination basis, with a maximum of eight sailors in each heat. Each race, even in the minimum prescribed wind, will only last a matter of minutes.

Other variations on slalom racing include "Man-on-Man" racing and "Open Ocean Slalom", both of which entail less gybing and longer legs. In this type of racing, the sailor's own board speed is of paramount importance over such long legs. Tactics, apart from the start itself, are less crucial than in normal slalom competitions, and so indeed are the gybing skills.

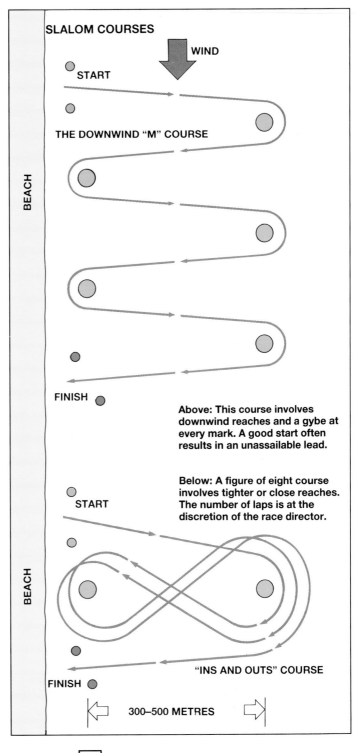

SLALOM COURSES

WIND

START

THE DOWNWIND "M" COURSE

BEACH

FINISH

Above: This course involves downwind reaches and a gybe at every mark. A good start often results in an unassailable lead.

Below: A figure of eight course involves tighter or close reaches. The number of laps is at the discretion of the race director.

START

BEACH

FINISH

"INS AND OUTS" COURSE

300–500 METRES

Slalom tactics

The tactical and strategic aspects of slalom are as simple to grasp as the nature of the course itself. All the action is fast and furious, leaving little time for thought.

The position regarding rules is much simpler than in course racing. In fact the rules hardly exist, bar one – an overtaking board must keep clear at all times, even if the competing sailor tries to luff up or bear down on him.

The start, again, is critical; an early lead is easy to retain, provided the sailor stays cool and out of trouble. The starting gate can be positioned either on the beach or on the water.

A beach or "Le Mans" start involves the competitors lining up on the water's edge, or just in the shallows. Position on the line is important, especially as the windward end is often favoured, with undisturbed wind and a broad reach to the first mark. To ensure fair play, lots are drawn to decide the line-up. Once the gun is fired, you must make as fast a beach start as possible. Run into the water and jump aboard when about knee deep. If you leap aboard too soon, the fin will ground, and you will catapult off the board. Once aboard, pump the rig to reach planing speed and try to get clear from the rest of the pack.

A start out at sea, between a committee boat and buoy, is sometimes preferred. Competitors must now decide whether the line has any bias, and try to avoid overcrowded areas. Your aim is to hit the line fully planing, a split second after the start gun goes off. Timing is of the essence here; too early a start and you will have to back off and risk stalling, too late and the pack will be away before you. Recalls, both individual and general, are common since competitors jockey for position.

After the start, your options are pretty limited. You must aim to get maximum board speed and stay out of trouble. If you have no one snapping at your heels, it's a good idea to head high in the beginning, so that you can bear down on the buoy. Beware that no one tries to

slip through to leeward. If you are heading up it will be difficult for them to pass you to windward. With any luck, you should arrive at the buoy on a broad reach, entering wide and leaving close to the buoy. The biggest danger is other competitors; if you enter wide it can leave a gap on the inside. If danger is imminent, then you must go for a close entry and a tight arced gybe to follow.

Advantage may be gained from a pile up at a mark. Your objective is to stay clear. An extremely precise gybe is needed to sweep through and bypass the casualties on the inside. If you are undecided, then play safe and take a very wide arc around the outside and immediately head up on exit to regain your line.

The slalom gybe

In all aspects of slalom competition, board speed is of paramount importance. A good start has its obvious advantages – few positions are exchanged during the reaches. The gybe is a point where a race can be won or lost, with much depending on the efficiency of gybe technique.

A good gybe can be measured by comparing the speed of entry against the exit speed; the object being to come out of the gybe with the same speed as at entry. As slalom has become increasingly competitive, a special carve gybing technique has evolved, with its own idiosyncracies, and quite distinct from a conventional carve gybe.

The trick is to maintain control at maximum board speed. In a conventional gybe, the sailor sheets out a little, to reduce speed and coax the board through a turn. In a slalom gybe, the sailor sheets in harder, thus presenting less sail to the wind. This enables him to keep control in the critical transition period, yet also maintain enough board speed and sail power to accelerate out of the turn, aided by a late rig flip.

Left: Prior to a gybe mark, it's essential to unhook and try to anticipate your turning arc.

Enter the turn at full speed looking for your line around the mark and a smooth area in which to turn. You will most likely be on a broad reach. Unhook from the harness, and move your back hand towards the rear boom end and oversheet the rig slightly, as you carve the board. Maintain plenty of mast foot pressure to keep the board level and plane as you pass the run point of sailing. You are still sailing clew-first at this point. As you exit onto the new reach, flip the rig and simultaneously change your feet – this should happen in a split second. You should now be balanced and ready to power up, without any loss of board speed. Hook in and go!

Familiarity with your equipment and prevailing conditions will dictate just how tight you can turn without loss of speed. Be aware of lulls in the wind which will slow your exit. On entry, watch for chop, especially in strong airs where the slightest bounce could upset your balance. The slalom gybe should be easy to grasp if you can already do a competent carve gybe.

In a race situation, other factors come into play to disturb the equilibrium. Among these are dirty air and turbulent water from other competitors. If you slow down on exit, due to distractions caused by other sailors, then try to get moving again as soon as possible. Pump away as soon as the sail is flipped, otherwise you may find others who have had a less troublesome turn, exiting on the plane and passing you for dead.

Surf slalom

To make things more interesting and exciting, slalom is sometimes run in challenging conditions, for example, incorporating gale-force winds and breaking surf. Here, the outer marks are set out to sea beyond the breaking waves, while the inner turn can be in the impact zone itself.

Sailing a slalom in surf is one of those situations where previous experience is invaluable. On the outward leg, the aim is to avoid sections of white water weaving up or correspondingly downwind to ensure a safe passage – a wipe-out in a wave will certainly mean exit from the competition. At all times, you must try to keep the board in contact with the water. Time in the air is wasted time, and can lose you positional advantage.

If a wave looms, you should anticipate a jump early. In most instances the racer can retract both legs, and by bending the knees, a jump can be dampened to almost nothing. Situations do arise when the speed of the slalom board and the steep wave make a jump inevitable. When faced with this, aim to project the board in a long flat arc, where control and speed in the air are at a premium. Watch out, on landing, for aerated water which follows the wave; this often leads to spin-out.

Concentrate on the inner gybes and keep a watchful eye on the wave behind you. Survival is the most important criterion. The wave that closes out or breaks behind you presents danger – especially if you are in mid-gybe. If the white water tumbles behind you, it may pay to gybe after it has broken. Much will depend on the conditions, and how your fellow competitors are faring.

Below: Sometimes in surf slalom jumps are unavoidable. To keep up speed, project the board in a long shallow-type jump.

Opposite top: Enter the slalom gybe at top planing speed – you should not be overpowered.

Opposite middle: With arms apart, lean into the gybe and oversheet slightly on entry.

Opposite bottom: As you come through the downwind stage, keep your body weight forward by using mast-foot pressure.

Top: Simultaneously swap your feet and flip the rig onto the new broad reach.

Above: Power out of the last sector of the turn at an exit speed close to that of entry.

CHAPTER 8

SPEEDSAILING

Throughout the ages men have been obsessed with speed, and windsurfing is no exception to this rule. Even in the infancy of the sport, speed was an important aspect of it. At that time the parameters were set, not surprisingly, by yacht racing authorities. The Royal Yachting Association of Great Britain held an annual competition for all types of sailing craft, in which a wide variety of weird and wonderful craft made a bid for the honour of breaking the speed record. These early events at Weymouth, on England's south coast, attracted windsurfing's early speed pioneers, including Britain's Clive Colenso who made his mark with a speed of 19.1 knots.

In those early days there was little in the way of electronic time-keeping, and windsurfing equipment was basic. The fastest sailors tended to be those with the most strength combined with body weight, who could hang on to a large sail in strong winds. Even so, it was not long before windsurfers eclipsed all other sailing craft in terms of speed. Today speed trials are held at many locations, such as Port St. Louis in southern France and Sotavento in the Canaries, and the majority of these are solely windsurf oriented. Recorded times now regularly achieve 30 to 40 knots, which would have been hard to imagine a mere decade ago.

Speed trials, perhaps more than any other aspect of windsurfing, rely on certain conditions to attain these exceptional top speeds. A strong wind, almost approaching a gale (35 knots and over) is a prerequisite. In such strong airs the normal sailing craft usually struggle to maintain control, while the windsurfer displays its true colours, eclipsing all other sailing craft to become the fastest in the world.

Right: A flash from the past when speed trials were boat oriented. Windsurfers are now dominating speedsailing records.

THE COMPETITIVE EDGE

The acid test for all aspiring speedsters is competition, whether it be against a rival or the clock. There are various kinds of speed competition, the best known being the RYA sanctioned events, organized to a strict set of rules.

Speed competition, with its enormous popularity, demands a special kind of mental attitude, as the individual makes the run solo and is, in the short term, only battling against the clock. At the end of the day, however, the rider has the rest of the speedsailors' times to consider and compete against.

For an official time to be ratified, an RYA observer must be present for the duration of an event. The observer's job is to oversee the organization, and to assure that there is fair play. The immediate prerequisites are that the course has an accurate timing system, and is 500 metres long (approx. 550 yards). Normally two transit posts are set up, and these act as sighting points for the timers, as well as start and finish marks for the sailors. The transits are set up geometrically by an independent surveyor to guarantee the course length. Timing is operated manually at each transit point, when the timer

punches a key on a computer. There may also be video time lapse cameras sighting each transit, against whose readings the times can later be checked for accuracy. The sailor's lapse time over the 500m is converted into metres per second, which in turn is converted to nautical miles per hour, or knots.

The world record must be beaten by two per cent in order to stand. This margin for error is a throwback from the pre-video timing days. Times that approach the record are entered onto a ranking list, which incorporates a sailor's personal bests from results obtained in similar competitions.

THE RIGHT CONDITIONS

There are many variables which combine to make a perfect speed venue. Foremost among these is the surface water condition. The flatter or smoother the water, the greater potential there will be for high speed sailing. Most people tend to know areas of tranquil seas from, perhaps, bathing or other flat water sports such as water skiing. However, when the wind picks up to ideal speedsailing strength, very few areas remain flat. For speedsailing, the best conditions occur on the windward shores of lakes or in coastal areas where the wind is offshore. Next to the shoreline there is only a short fetch for the offshore wind, irrespective of strength, to disturb the water. Even at 110yds (100m) offshore, the wind-blown chop will be enough to hamper control. The further offshore, the stronger the wind and the greater the fetch for waves to build up. The sailor may get the impression that he is going really fast, when in reality he may be just fighting with the chop.

Just as important as the water is the wind itself. Speedsailing, more than any other aspect of the sport, needs strong wind. Around 20 knots is the bare minimum to even start the largest of speedboards. Ideally, the speed freak is looking for winds in excess of 35 knots.

Competitions are organized to coincide, as much as possible, with

expected breezes. Events are either calendared to trade winds, which are often reliable, or to seasons of stormy weather. It can be, however, a bit of a lottery relying on weather systems.

Not only does the wind have to be blowing hard, it also has to be clean. By clean, we mean relatively constant and free from obstacles which may disrupt its flow. With so little volume in speed-needles, a slight lull or wind shadow in the lee of a building can give the speedster that awful sinking feeling! The classic example of clean wind may be found at the famous Sotavento course, in Fuerteventura (Canary Islands), where the wind blows undisturbed across a kilometre of flat beach before it shoots offshore.

For serious speedsailing, it is important that the course be at the correct angle relative to the wind. All points of reaching are fast, but the broad reach is the quickest. A course set across the wind, beam reach at 90°, is inherently slower than a course greater than 90° off the wind. The optimum angle for record breaking is between 130 and 140° off the wind. A good stiff

Right: For optimum performance the leading sailor has taken the inside, flat water line. Take note of how much distance the sailor, who is following behind him, has left in order to get undisturbed wind and water.

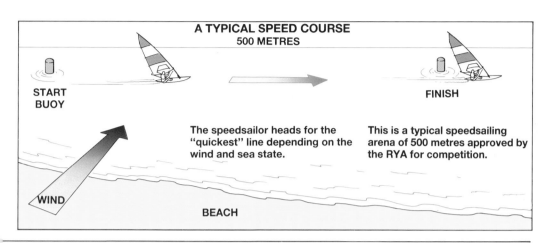

A TYPICAL SPEED COURSE
500 METRES

START BUOY

FINISH

The speedsailor heads for the "quickest" line depending on the wind and sea state.

This is a typical speedsailing arena of 500 metres approved by the RYA for competition.

WIND

BEACH

breeze is required to blow along the speedster so far off the wind. In certain locations, the organizers have the ability to run a series of courses to achieve the perfect incidence angle of wind. Brest, in northern France, is probably the best example of this. The course can be run through any diameter of a circle, with transit points rather like a clockface. Unfortunately there is a price to pay for keeping so many options open; this course can not be set on a windward shoreline, and the water surface is therefore choppy.

It is difficult to satisfy all the speedsailing requirements of the course length, wind, flat water and wind angle. Natural speedsailing venues are few and far between. To reduce the variables of flat water and wind angle, man-made speed courses have been built. These courses, resembling canals, obviously have flat water and are directed across prevailing winds. Recently they have had extensive use for private trials, where only invited sailors can compete with the sole object of mounting an assault on the record.

Fortunately there are other ways in which windsurfers can satisfy their appetite for speed. One of the most popular of these is the short course of 100 or 250m (approx. 110 or 275yds). Short courses bring many other venues into play where, for example, it would be impossible to fit in the regulation 500m. It is easier to achieve higher speeds on these short courses, as maximum velocity has to be sustained for only a fraction of the time. Local events, run to a tight budget, can benefit from short courses, as they can be set up almost instantly and with the help of volunteers, at almost no cost. However, there can be no official ratification of speed on such a course.

There are other low cost alternatives – the "friend and stopwatch" approach – timing between two buoys set at a known distance apart. Becoming increasingly popular are speedtraps, as used by police forces, where the sailor is "shot" by a "speed cop" using a conventional speedgun.

SAILING THE COURSE

Getting the maximum benefit from a speed course, during a trial, is not quite as straightforward as it may appear. Luck plays an important role, yet there are ways of giving it a helping hand!

Let us first consider the start. In many trials there is a bit of a battle to reach the line and get the right to make a run. If competitors are sensible and either wait in line or stagger themselves to the start, everyone will get a reasonable crack of the whip. It's imperative to cross the imaginary start line at full speed, otherwise the time, when averaged out over the total distance, will suffer.

Remember that the flattest water is always nearest to the shoreline. So, provided the wind is good in this area, take the inside line as close as you dare!

Keep a watchful eye on the water ahead. Even the slightest lump or bump can bring about a loss of control at high speed. A resulting spin-out or catapult over the board could easily damage more than just your ego!

Always keep alert for other sailors. Keep your distance from the competitor in front of you. If a sailor wipes out, it may be too late to stop or alter course. Following closely will also mean riding in a choppy wake with dirty air from the preceding sailor, which will certainly reduce your speed.

The wind rarely stays constant over the whole length of the course. Gusts can actually be used to favour the speedsailor. They can be foreseen (as can lulls) by observing the surface condition – the sailor must be prepared to act fast. Get ready to take the strain of a strong gust in your stride, otherwise it will whip you over the nose of the board. To gain extra speed, bear off slightly on the gust, and the board will accelerate. Similarly, if you spot a lull, head up a touch, otherwise you will run out of power. Be aware that there can be a change of wind direction on a gust; rarely, however, do these lifts and headers affect the speedsailor. Speedsailing is a matter of flowing with the wind, and not of following a dead straight line from transit to transit. Try to get as many runs in as possible.

Opposite: Australian Peter Dans sailing the course at Sotavento, Fuerteventura. Competitors travel from all four corners of the earth to sail in the more prestigious events. Under such circumstances, competition and rivalry is intense.

Below: Catapults are all too common in contests and during training. Sometimes these wipe-outs are a result of an error in judgement – not anticipating a gust or sailing too hard on choppy water.

TUNE-UP TIME

It's not much use having good equipment if it's not set up correctly. Poorly tuned kit is rather like a misfiring car. There are things one can do to help matters. The surface of the hull, for example, can be smoothed to a fine finish. An application of wet and dry papers will improve the board's hygroscopic characteristics. Harsh, gritty papers are not recommended, as they may score the hull unduly.

To aid water flow, the fin box is commonly filled in around the fin, which also reduces the chances of aeration from the box. The water, when it hits the fin, is undisturbed giving less resistance, and less likelihood of spinning out.

The mast track should be situated far aft. This will reduce the board's wetted area while planing off the wind. The reduction in drag speaks for itself. On speedneedles, the mast foot lies between 58 and 62ins (147 and 157cm) from the tail, depending on the wind direction and strength.

Often, too little consideration is given to tuning up the sail. For high speeds the sail should be set shallow, with less drag, rather than full. Although a fuller sail has excellent acceleration, its top end speed is not so good. The tack of the sail needs to be set sufficiently close to the deck, so that the slot between board and sail is shut off early. The efficiency of the rig depends very largely on this consideration – any gap creates turbulence which will reduce it drastically.

In strong airs a sail's stability can often be less than perfect. The draught can easily move fore and aft as the rig distorts under load. Locking the centre of effort is directly related to downhaul tension. In high winds the rule is: the more downhaul, the better.

If these few pointers are followed, and you are still not going any faster, then there's probably something wrong with your sailing technique. For speed, it is necessary to develop an upright stance. A low boom set at chest level, and a seat harness should assist this stance. Be sure not to set the lines

too long otherwise you will not gain the correct leverage on the rig. If possible, maintain a firm body posture and hold the sail as rigidly as you can. A sharp rig or boom movement will easily disturb the status quo.

It is vital to react to any undulations in the track. To do this, keep your rear leg bent with its weight pushing down through the fin, as opposed to against it. This bent limb can act as a shock absorber, reducing the effect of the chop on the board's trim.

Below: A typical speedsail in motion. Many sails incorporate four of five camber-inducers plus the head and foot batten.

Above: A drop cleat enables the sail to be set close and secure to the deck, to a point below the mast base itself.

TANDEMS AND TRIDEMS

Windsurfing has an extravagant side to it, which is best indicated by multi-rigged crafts. When they first appeared, tandems were treated as quite a joke. Then suddenly in 1986, France's Bertin and Griessman burst through the 30 knot barrier at Port St. Louis in southern France – tandems were no longer a laughing matter.

Speed tandems are exceptionally difficult to waterstart. However, once a team of sailors is co-ordinated, the task becomes much easier. As soon as the board is up and running, control is less of a problem to worry about. The attraction of team-work is self-evident, as more and more tandems make their presence felt and achieve respectable times. Many feel that, intrinsically, tandems may be faster than solo boards.

The three man or tridem board must be looked at more as a curiosity rather than a serious challenger for anything. A waterstart, tack or gybe is virtually unheard of here, and a wipe-out correspondingly time consuming. It can't be denied, however, that such odd machines have a great deal of spectator appeal.

Below: The tridem or three man board reflects the true meaning of team-work. Launching, and indeed stopping, is an art unto itself. In competition the tridem has not, as yet, eclipsed its tandem cousin, although it has attained respectable speed.

STARTING A SPEED-NEEDLE

A waterstart is the only way of get-ting aboard anything that resem-bles a speedboard, whether 17ins (43cm) wide or a spear-like 11½ins (29cm) wide. Due to the board's natural low volume, this technique has to be modified. Even a compe-tent shortboarder could struggle to get aboard if not familiar with the speed-needle.

The first step is identical to a normal waterstart. Get the board across the wind and fly the rig. Watch out in case the often light-weight board flips over as the rig clears the water. Place either one or both feet ahead of their respective footstraps. Raise the rig to create lift, keeping hands well back on the boom, and then start getting on. The board will still be pointing sky-wards; you should hang on and apply heavy mast-foot pressure. Encourage the board up by working the rig and bearing away – this can be an exhausting process. Keep pumping until you are on the plane

1. **The first move, as with any waterstart, is to fly the rig. Be careful, as a speedboard can invert very easily.**

2. **Raise the rig and get as close to the board as possible. Place either your front or rear foot on the board.**

3. **In order to create enough lift: raise the rig as high as you can and surge out of the water in an explosive motion.**

4. **Once aboard hang onto the rig's power, bearing away to try and float the sunken board. This part can cause a lot of strain.**

5. **Continue to bear away and pump the rig to get the board planing. Be careful not to oversheet and stall.**

6. **Only when you are confident that the board is well up and running should you enter both sets of footstraps, and hook into the harness.**

1.

2.

3.

4.

5.

6.

– this may take some effort to achieve. Place your front and then rear foot in their straps, and hook in to the harness to rest your arms.

It is important to keep both feet over the board's centre line in order not to upset the trim. On many narrow needles, it is often necessary to align your feet along the line of the board otherwise the spray they create, until fully planing, may be unbearable. Waterstarting small boards not only requires sound technique, but also fitness. The hardest part is getting the board to unstick itself onto the plane.

With larger speedboards it is sometimes possible to start with a foot already in a strap. This can rarely be said of their narrower counterparts unless the wind approaches a gale.

Below: Speedboards come in an array of sizes. Recreational boards tend to be wider, up to 19ins (48cm), while full record-breakers can be as narrow as a spear-like 10ins (25cm).

CHAPTER 9

STATE OF THE ART

High-performance windsurfing has come a long way in the past five years. Not so long ago, such moves as 360s, jump gybes and forward rolls would have seemed almost an impossibility. Many of these moves were the result of accident, rather than design, and being able to repeat a man-oeuvre twice in succession was more a matter of good fortune than judgement.

It is now possible to set about most of these radical moves in a methodical way; technological advances combined with better teaching methods have worked wonders, resulting in a level of performance that, only recently, would have seemed miraculous.

At the highest level of the sport, new moves are often emulated within hours of their inception. Total commitment, combined with a competitive spirit, and that famous "go for it!" attitude have raised performance to very high levels.

A word of warning to the less expert – an adventurous attitude has its dangers. Unless the move you are attempting is somewhere within your range of achievement, leave it well alone. Injuries usually result from a daredevil approach coupled with poor control. The proper way to progression is step by step, and you take short cuts at your peril.

Don't be unduly alarmed, however. It is only at the very top end of the sport that the limits are being pushed in a way that might involve danger to life and limb. Generally speaking, windsurfing is still one of the safest sports provided common sense prevails. By all means go for it! Remember, however, that this attitude can be well thought out giving you a chance of success, or uncalculated leaving you no chance of survival.

Right: This one-handed jump gybe is pure showmanship, it can be executed hooked in or out, the first is your easier bet.

ONE-HANDED JUMPS

If you are reasonably proficient at jumping, a one-handed jump should be well within your grasp. You have the option of either releasing the front or rear hand – both methods are acceptable. Of little practical use, it is a stylish way of exhibiting good control.

This process is executed hooked in to the harness lines. It is essential that your lines are set perfectly, otherwise the sail will head into or away from the wind. Long jumps are the best to try.

Approach the ramp as you would a normal jump. On take-off, remain hooked and sheeted in to gain maximum height. While still on the way up, release one hand (in this case the front one) and show it to the crowd. Keep sheeted in, while still keeping your other hand free. As you descend, bring the tail of the board slightly to windward. Immediately prior to splash-down, return the free hand to grip the boom. The landing may be harder than normal – so be prepared.

After take-off, you may, alternatively, release your rear hand. At this juncture, many sailors draw the board up with a bent rear leg and grab the fin or the tail. This tail grab is a natural aid to flight control, since it automatically forces the board into a good flight path.

It is essential in all these jumps to retain full control. If you hook out of the harness line, the sail will depower, and you'll drop awkwardly. Try to land the board nose first. This is easier said than done, since landings are often heavy and sometimes flat. Continued front-hand releases can often be damaging to your board, especially when you land badly from a great height.

A final point to bear in mind – be aware of the potential catapult on landing. To land, you must have both hands securely on the boom and your mind on the job. A lapse of concentration in mid-flight could make you experience the wipe-out of a lifetime!

Far left: Approach the ramp fully planing as if entering a normal jump, however, you must remain hooked into the harness.

Left: As you leave the wave, release your front hand and show it to the crowd. A long flat or chop hop jump should follow.

Far left below: Position the board slightly downwind using only foot pressure to do this. Keep your hand out at the high point of the jumping process.

Left below: While on your way down, return the loose hand back to the boom.

Below: The tail grab jump is a popular form of one-handed jumps. It helps, in this instance, to leave the wave before releasing the back hand. You then have a choice of either waving the hand, or retracting the board by bending your rear leg to grab the tail momentarily.

AERIAL DUCK GYBE

There are not many transitions that come into the radical category. First to be perfected was the aerial gybe, closely followed by the duck gybe version.

The idea is relatively simple: jump the board and, in mid-flight, pass the boom over your head and proceed to the new tack. Needless to say, it's not that easy in practice!

Initiate the transition by planing on a broad reach heading for a small wave or chop to create lift. With your back foot out of the strap, chop hop and push the tail downwind. Commence the duck gybe by moving your front hand to the rear boom end, simultaneously switching your feet in flight. As you and the board pass through the eye of the wind, throw the rig over your shoulder.

Passing the rig over your head is easy – catching it is a different matter. For a split second, you have to release the rig completely in order to reach for the boom beyond its balance point. If you are still aboard at this point, hang on tight, because hitting the water is liable to be a nose first and forceful affair. A quick start should round things off very nicely.

The overall success rate for this move is pretty minimal, so don't be too discouraged by repeated failed attempts. In high wind they usually result in the rig being blown violently downwind, closely followed by both board and sailor.

Below: During higher attempts, it's difficult to grasp the rig and hold on. The usual course of action automatically follows.

Right: The rig change during an aerial duck gybe is exactly the same as a regular duck gybe, except it's done while airborne.

FORWARD LOOP

The full forward – or "killer" – loop (as it is sometimes known) is one of the most spectacular manoeuvres that windsurfing has to offer. In some ways it resembles the forward roll, and the two are often confused by the spectator. In fact the loop evolved from the roll, and requires an entirely different technique. If you can imagine a roll being a horizontal corkscrew motion, then the loop may be described as a vertical cart-wheel action.

The best conditions for a forward loop are side-shore winds and a reasonable 5 to 6½ft (1.5 to 2m) take-off ramp. Approach the wave heading for a good steep section to gain maximum lift. Decide on your course of action before taking off. The first movement is a chop hop, gaining as much height as possible off the wave. At the apex of the jump, oversheet the rig until you are almost bearing away in mid-air. The

1.

2.

3.

nose of the board will dive dramatically downwind – aid the rotation by leaning forward. The board will lift through the wind and totally invert – hold on tight! The remainder of the loop is a vertical fall back onto the water. If the rotation is achieved correctly, you will land almost level on the board.

The main problems occur in the preliminary stages of this move. You must remember to jump first and *then* lean, otherwise you'll end up doing more of an inverted roll. Make a conscious effort to grip your board firmly, or else your feet will slip out as the rotation starts. Continue to be completely committed

throughout, since a partial rotation is more than likely to result in a head butt of the mast.

In cases where the take-off ramp is small, the mast tip may catch the water on the way over. If you stay alert and dexterous, you can complete a pole-vault motion to continue the loop.

4.

As seen in the five steps illustrated here, carry out the forward loop manoeuvre by immediately chop hopping off the wave while keeping the sail **sheeted in hard (1). Then bear away in the air extending both front hand and leg (2). The sail will catch the wind and power the board around (3). Hang on tight –** **as the sail pivots, the mast may catch the water (4). The mast tip will release and flick you down to earth (5). It is easy to spot your landing as you take-off.**

5.

FLAT WATER LOOP

Experienced forward rollers and loopers know that, by adapting the style slightly, the manoeuvre can be performed to good effect on smaller ramps. It is possible to evolve a method which can be adapted to loop on the way in to the shore, off the back of a wave, or even on completely flat water.

Although the flat water loop is executed only a hair's breadth off the water surface, don't suppose this necessarily means that it's safe! In fact, success is less assured than a similar move attempted off a waveface. The speed of rotation is so great, that a mistake becomes disaster in a split second.

The secret of success is board speed, so before even attempting it, you must be at full bore on a broad reach. Look for the slightest ramp or bump to gain air. In an explosive action, chop hop for all you're worth to gain maximum clearance. Sheet in and lean forward; it helps to really exaggerate the movement. As the board nose dives, continue to lean. The nose may even skim the water before the rotation creates further lift.

To create enough lift the wind needs to be strong, in fact, the stronger, the better – Force 5.

As soon as you're airborne, initiate the move; time is of the essence at this point. All too often there is not enough clearance left for a clean landing, but provided the rotation has been achieved, you should land safely in the water.

With practice, these low rotation loops and rolls can be executed on the waveface itself. It is helpful to initiate the move at the wave's base in order to reduce the chance of the wave engulfing you upon landing.

Right: Even if the water is perfectly flat, it's possible to perform a roll or loop.

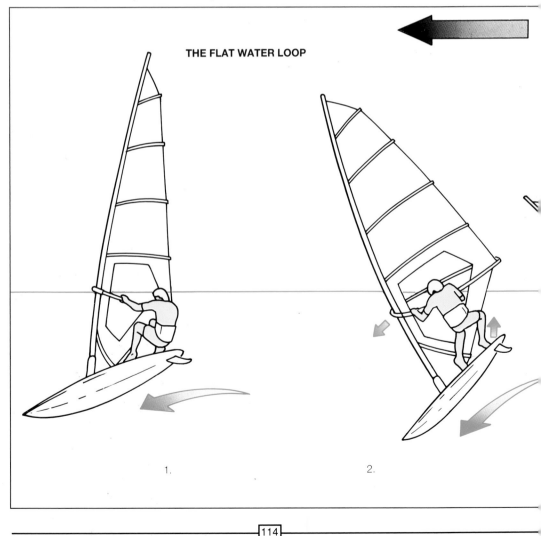

THE FLAT WATER LOOP

1.

2.

1. Head full speed on a broad reach. It can help to be a little overpowered. Do your best jump.

2. Sheet in hard and lean forward – attempt to really exaggerate this movement.

3. The board's nose will flick through the wind, catching the water to pivot you round tighter.

4. Grip the board tight with your feet and, hopefully, you should make it onto the new reach.

3.

4.

GU SCREW

Although the Gu screw action appears as a jump, it is, in fact, a waveriding manoeuvre named after its Hawaiian based inventor – Mark Angulo. The right conditions for a Gu screw are a steep waveface combined with a strong cross-offshore wind. This manoeuvre relies much on speed of take-off. The cross-off wind facilitates maximum board speed along the waveface. The technical merit of this rotating motion is extremely high.

While fully planing, almost overpowered, shoot along the waveface at top speed, downwind. Carve up sharply towards the lip of the wave, as if to shoot over the back of it. You will leave the wave clew-first. Lean in towards the turn.

The wind should catch the clew to aid rotation. If you have spun fast enough, you should most probably land tail first on the inwards tack – it's impossible to land back onto the waveface.

Without actually seeing the Gu screw performed, it is difficult to visualize. Unlike some other moves, the difficulty factor far outweighs the apparent danger. The somewhat strange rotation calls for real dexterity. The secret is all in the take-off process. Rake the rig in towards your hip with the front hand, to present more clew and increased leverage for the wind.

Another move of similar aspect is the Kalama roll named after its American inventor, Dave Kalama. This is, broadly speaking, a forward roll over the back of the wave, again landing behind the ramp. The best conditions for attempting this are when the wind is strongly offshore. High board speed is required. The Kalama roll incorporates a hop right up by the lip, where the board should be almost parallel to the wave. This is followed by a forward roll into the trough. Be aware of the strong gust behind the wave in the cross-offshore breezes.

Right: The Gu screw is a difficult concept to grasp. Initiate the manoeuvre by carving up and out of the wave following a fast bottom turn.

Far right: On coming out of the wave, point the nose of the board up into the wind by extending your front leg and bearing away in the air.

Below right: The wind should catch the sail's clew and assist the rotation, flicking the board to point back towards the shore.

Below far right: Usually you'll land with the rig upright – be aware of probable gusts on touchdown. Due to the nature of the rotation, you'll always land in the trough!

Below: Here we see the mid-point of a Kalama roll. The sailor has shot off the wave, after a bottom turn, to perform a roll.

ONE-HANDED LOOP

With forward rotations now commonplace, radical sailors have had to look for new challenges. The one-handed roll or loop is perhaps their way of throwing down the gauntlet to other competitors. The immediate prerequisites are a good steep ramp and lots of wind. Before taking off, you should make your mind up on whether it's to be a roll or a loop – either is open to you. It should be executed with the use of a harness.

Approach the wave on a broad reach, hooked in at full speed. Release your rear hand and begin the rolling motion well before take-off. As you take off, lean hard to get on top of the rig. The wind alone will take you over, but use your free arm to give extra momentum. You should splash down while still gripping the rig in a starting position.

To have any chance of living to tell the tale, you must be totally proficient in performing a normal roll or loop. The most difficult area is getting the momentum of the

initial rotation going. It's so easy to go up and just stop halfway – this is a good recipe for a boom or sail "sandwich". For initial attempts, it is better to keep both hands on the boom, still hooked in, to start the rotating motion. You can then release the rear hand to achieve a similar but detuned result.

The one-handed variations can also be performed on the way in to the shore, normally off the back of a wave. However, to gain sufficient height it helps to be blowing at least a Force 6.

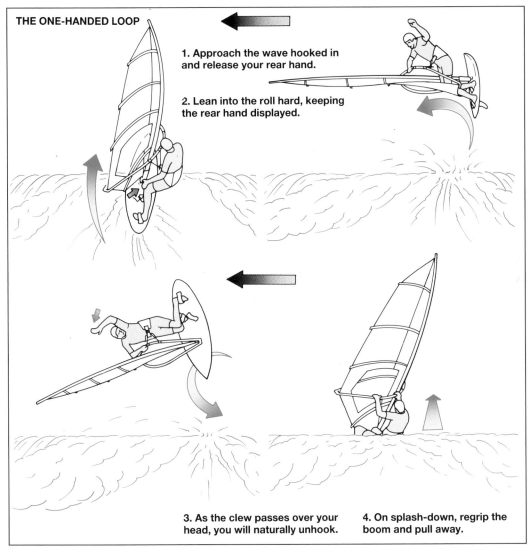

THE ONE-HANDED LOOP

1. Approach the wave hooked in and release your rear hand.

2. Lean into the roll hard, keeping the rear hand displayed.

3. As the clew passes over your head, you will naturally unhook.

4. On splash-down, regrip the boom and pull away.

VARIATIONS ON THE THEME

Although some of the aforementioned manoeuvres may appear the ultimate in funboard sailing, they are by no means the end of the road. New moves and variations are continually being dreamed up and put into practice. What we have covered in the foregoing pages is merely a selection of some of the more popular moves that are currently on offer.

The list of possibilities is endless – head dip jumps, one-footed jumps, double loops and even one hand with one foot loops. And who would have thought, just a season ago, that the one-handed jump would be superseded by a no-handed version of virtually the same jump? These moves are not just pie in the sky, they are actually being performed, more or less, on a daily basis in such highly competitive locations such as Maui in Hawaii, western Australia and the Canary Islands.

The key to all these moves is practice. Careful study of the techniques involved will certainly reduce the learning curve. It quickly becomes apparent that many moves are the base of others. For full enjoyment and safety, try and hold a full repertoire of the essential base building blocks.

"Whatever will come next?" one wonders. Only time will tell!

Below: Here a no-handed jump performed at Sprecklesville, Maui, home of many of the latest high-profile moves.

119

GLOSSARY

aerial a manoeuvre which is performed clear of the water surface, e.g. "aerial gybe".

aerial off-the-lip a top turn manoeuvre where the board hops off the face of the wave and then comes back down to land on the same face.

apparent wind a combination of the true wind and the headwind created by forward motion.

asymmetric a board which has been designed with each side having contrasting characteristics. Best used in consistent wave conditions. One side is extended into a long drawn out shape for fast turns at the bottom of the wave, while the other side is wider for slower, sharper turns off the top of the wave.

barrel roll a variation of the backward loop; the most traditional of all the various forms of loop.

beam reach sailing at right angles to the wind.

bear away to change course; turning the board away from the wind.

bottom turn a turn which is made at the bottom of the waveface, after which the board is projected towards the top.

broad reach the fastest point of sailing, half-way between a beam reach and a run, where the wind is directly behind.

camber-inducer a fork shaped moulding which attaches the sail batten to the mast, enabling the sail to rotate smoothly while creating a perfect camber. Mostly used for power and speed.

cantagalli roll the forward roll looping movement named after its inventor, Italian sailor Cesare Cantagalli.

carve to turn the board sharply by pressing the inside rail.

centre of effort an imaginary central point in the sail through which the power is generated.

chop small wind-blown waves.

close out the wave breaks all the way along its length.

critical section the section of the wave which is closest to the breaking white water.

cut-back a turning manoeuvre performed on the shoulder of the wave, where the board is projected back into the pocket near to the breaking section.

donkey kick a variation of the "table top". Sometimes known as the "mule kick".

drop in to launch from the peak of the wave and drop down the face.

gu screw radical waveriding manoeuvre named after its Hawaiian based inventor, Mark Angulo.

head up or "luff up" means to guide the board up into the wind.

helicopter a shortboard freestyle transition designed to impress the judges.

impact zone the area to avoid, between the oncoming waves and the shore, where waves break the hardest.

killer loop common term for the full forward loop. Windsurfing's most spectacular aerial manoeuvre.

leech the trailing edge of the sail.

leeward the side of the board or sail which is furthest away from the wind.

luff the leading edge of the sail.

marginal a board which will float when not in motion but begin to sink when the rig is uphauled.

mast-foot pressure exertion on the rig going into the board.

off-the-lip a turn performed off the critical top section of the wave, projecting the board down the face of the wave.

peak the highest point on the waveface.

rails the sides of the board.

re-entry a snappy frontside top turn performed on the breaking section of the wave.

rocker the amount of curvature throughout the length of the board.

rotational the RAF (Rotating Asymmetric Foil) system was originated by Barry Spanier and Geoff Bourne (sailmakers on the Hawaiian island of Maui). The system allows the battens to rotate freely around the mast to create a clean foil shape.

sinker a board which cannot support the sailor's weight when stationary.

slot the area between the foot of the sail and the deck of the board.

speed-needle low volume boards specifically designed for speed trials, often as narrow as a mere 11½ins (29cms) wide.

spin-out a problem often encountered when sailing fast in choppy waters. The surface area of the fin becomes aerated, causing it to lose grip, resulting in the board sliding sideways.

table top a jumping manoeuvre which entails twisting the bottom of the hull skywards.

"v" the shape across the bottom of the hull stretching from rail to rail.

waterstart the method for starting a board from a prone position in the water.

windward the side which is upwind or nearest to the wind.

wipe-out to fall from the board and lose control.

SHORTBOARD AND SAIL EXPLAINED

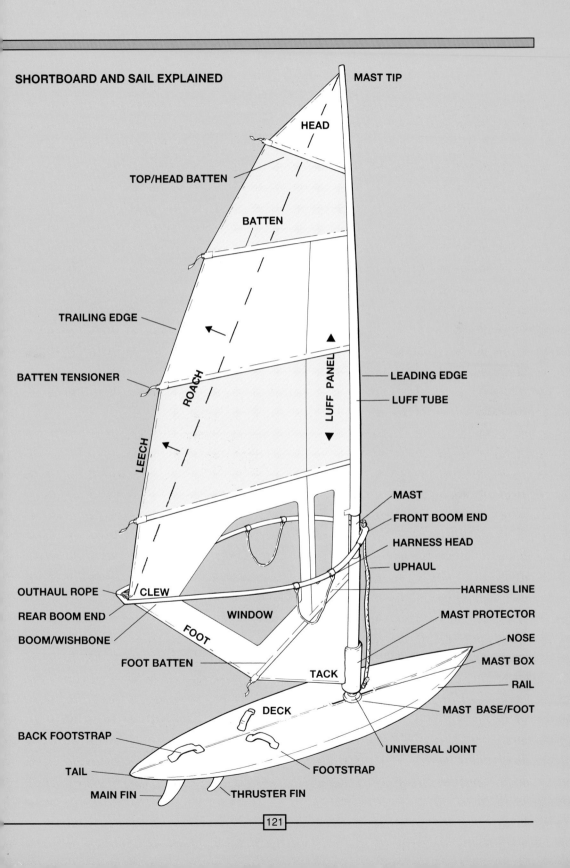

MAST TIP

HEAD

TOP/HEAD BATTEN

BATTEN

TRAILING EDGE

ROACH

LUFF PANEL

LEADING EDGE

LUFF TUBE

BATTEN TENSIONER

LEECH

MAST

FRONT BOOM END

HARNESS HEAD

UPHAUL

OUTHAUL ROPE

CLEW

HARNESS LINE

REAR BOOM END

WINDOW

MAST PROTECTOR

BOOM/WISHBONE

FOOT

NOSE

MAST BOX

FOOT BATTEN

TACK

RAIL

DECK

MAST BASE/FOOT

BACK FOOTSTRAP

UNIVERSAL JOINT

TAIL

FOOTSTRAP

MAIN FIN

THRUSTER FIN

INDEX

Numbers in *italics* refer to illustrations

A

aerial
  gybe 67
  off-the-lip 74, *75*
aluminium masts 21
anticyclones 40
armour 25, 52
aspect ratio of sails 18
asymmetrics 17

B

barrel roll 12, 80–1
battens 11, 12–13, 20
  tensioning 26–7
beach start 92
Beale, Eric 13
Beaufort Scale 40–1
board
  bag 25
  carrying 37–8
  designs 14–18
  early 8–10
  tuning up 102
body drag 66
boom 22
  buffers 25
  positioning 26
boots 24
bottom turn 70–1
Bourne, Geoff 10

C

Cabrinha, Peter *12*
camber-inducer 13
Cantagalli, Cesare 13, 82
carrying the gear 37–8
carve gybe 10, 34–6, *54*
  one-handed 36–7
catapult *101*
chop hop 76–7
clothing 23–4
course racing 86–90
  board design 16–17
coursesails 18
currents 42–3
custom boards 13, 14
cyclones 40

D

daggerboards 16–17
Dans, Peter *101*

derigging 27
  at sea *52*
downhaul 26, 27
drag, body 66
draught of sail 19
dual batten system 20
duck gybe 10, 56–7
  aerial 110
  one-handed 57–8
duck tack 65

E

edges *see* rails
epoxy resins 14–15
equipment checking 52

F

fibreglass boards 14
  masts 21
fin-box tuning 102
fins 21
flat water loop 114–15
flattened triangle course, 86, *87*
fog 42
footbatten 12–13
footstraps 8, 16, 17, 23
forward
  loop 112–13
  roll 13, 82–3
fronts 40

G

gloves 24
grips 21
Gu screw 116
gybe
  aerial 67
  carve 10, 34–7, *54*
  duck 10, 56–8
  jump, one-handed *106*
  onto wave 70
  slalom 93–4
  slam 60–1

H

hard sails 20
harnesses 24
Haywood, Fred 11
hazards 13
heat loss 23, 24
helicopter 62–3
helmets 13, 25
Honscheid, Jürgen 10, *11*
Horgan, Mike 8
Hunt, Doug 12
hydrodynamics 16
hypothermia 23, 52

I

inducers 20
ins and outs 91

J

jump boards 8–9
jumps 76–83
  gybe, one-handed *106*
  one-handed 109
  slalom 95

K

Kailua Kids 8, *9*
Kaiama roll 116
killer loop *see* forward loop

L

laminating, hand *15*
launching 38–9
Le Mans start 92
lightning 42
lines 24
loop
  flat water 114–15
  forward 112–13
  one-handed 118
  windward 12
luff curve 18

M

M course 91
Maka. Pascal 13
man-on-man 91
mast 21
  bend *see* luff curve
  pad 25
  stiffness 27–8
  tuning 102
Maui Sails 10
mists 42

N

Naish, Robby *9*
neap tide 42
neoprene boots 24
nose
  tack 62–3
  width 16

O

off-the-lip 72, *73*
  aerial 74, *75*
Olympics 12

W

Acknowledgements

Without the help of leading manufacturers within the sport of windsurfing, the industry and myself would not be in the respected position we are today. I would like to give my regards to: Roger and Hyjumpers for their infinite windsurfing accessories, Ross and Stuart at Sola Wetsuits, Chris, Johnathon and Katie at Grange Sports, Lightwave, Roger and Mickey at Tushingham for their full-bodied sails, Peter Newbold-Newman at Outback and Tradewind.

I would like to give special thanks to Paul Davies for his invaluable help in typing and rephrasing my Irish English, Math Medd for his advice on tides and weather and Justin Hooper-Greenhill for his advice and help on course racing. I would also like to thank Max Earey, Mike O'Brien, Cliff Webb at MX and Jono Knight for their photography. Last but not least, I would like to express my gratitude to Roseanne Eckart for her patience and efforts in helping to produce this book.

Farrel O'Shea